Country Woodcraft Patterns

Country Woodcraft Patterns

128 Patterns & Projects

■ ■ ■

Charles & Doris Pugh

Sterling Publishing Co., Inc. New York

Library of Congress Cataloging-in-Publication Data

Pugh, Charles (Charles W.)
    Country woodcraft patterns / by Charles and Doris Pugh.
       p.   cm.
    Includes index.
    1. Woodwork. I. Pugh, Doris. II. Title.
    TT180.P84 1990
    684'.08—dc20   90-39880
                                       CIP

10 9 8 7 6 5 4 3 2

Sterling ISBN 0-8069-7360-9

CONTENTS

Color section follows page 64

Metric Equivalents

INCHES TO MILLIMETRES AND CENTIMETRES

MM—millimetres   *CM—centimetres*

Inches	MM	CM	Inches	CM	Inches	CM
⅛	3	0.3	9	22.9	30	76.2
¼	6	0.6	10	25.4	31	78.7
⅜	10	1.0	11	27.9	32	81.3
½	13	1.3	12	30.5	33	83.8
⅝	16	1.6	13	33.0	34	86.4
¾	19	1.9	14	35.6	35	88.9
⅞	22	2.2	15	38.1	36	91.4
1	25	2.5	16	40.6	37	94.0
1¼	32	3.2	17	43.2	38	96.5
1½	38	3.8	18	45.7	39	99.1
1¾	44	4.4	19	48.3	40	101.6
2	51	5.1	20	50.8	41	104.1
2½	64	6.4	21	53.3	42	106.7
2	76	7.6	22	55.9	43	109.2
3½	89	8.9	23	58.4	44	111.8
4	102	10.2	24	61.0	45	114.3
4½	114	11.4	25	63.5	46	116.8
5	127	12.7	26	66.0	47	119.4
6	152	15.2	27	68.6	48	121.9
7	178	17.8	28	71.1	49	124.5
8	203	20.3	29	73.7	50	127.0

INTRODUCTION

A few simple tools and a little patience are all you need to create the many useful and attractive accessories you will find in this book. The patterns and complete instructions for assembly are included for each project. So, just choose a design, collect your materials and get started! We know you will enjoy the creating and your family and friends will love the results.

GENERAL INFORMATION

Lumber

When buying lumber such as a 1 × 8″ or a 1 × 10″, the actual size of the wood piece is somewhat smaller than the nominal size as indicated in the table below. (Actual size is used to specify board length.)

NOMINAL SIZE	ACTUAL SIZE
1″ × 2″	3/4″ × 1 1/2″
1″ × 3″	3/4″ × 2 1/2″
1″ × 4″	3/4″ × 3 1/2″
1″ × 5″	3/4″ × 4 1/2″
1″ × 6″	3/4″ × 5 1/2″
1″ × 8″	3/4″ × 7 1/4″
1″ × 10″	3/4″ × 9 1/4″
1″ × 12″	3/4″ × 11 1/4″

Lumber is classified as *select* or *common* based on its exterior appearance. Each classification is then subdivided by grades (1,2,3) with the highest grade, No. 1, being the most expensive. Common lumber should be adequate for the projects in this book; however, examine each piece of wood you purchase to determine that sufficient lengths of unblemished pieces can be cut to complete the design selected. Buying common lumber that you have screened can significantly reduce the cost of your project. Also, softwoods such as pine or fir are less expensive than the hardwoods like oak, birch or maple.

Plywood

Plywood is available in 4′ × 8′ sheets. Some lumber stores will sell smaller sizes at a higher price per square foot, such as 2′ × 4′. The thickness of plywood is given as actual size. Thicknesses generally available are 1/8″, 1/4″, 3/8″, 1/2″, 5/8″, 3/4″ and 1″.

Like lumber, plywood is graded according to its external appearance. Each side is individually graded from A to D with A being the highest grade. The higher the grade the higher the cost. For designs included in this book, softwood plywood is adequate, with the grade being determined by the desired appearance. For example, for a hanging display, the side which shows should be grade A and the side to the wall can be grade C. If both sides are visible you may want to buy A-A grade, or by screening the available sheets you may find a piece of lower grade that will work and save on the cost. If the finished unit is to be exposed to moisture or weather, use plywood with weatherproof glue (outdoor) only.

Glue

When the piece is to be used indoors, use the *white* (polyvinyl) or *yellow* (aliphatic resin) glues available in plastic bottles, such as Elmer's Wood Glue, when gluing is recommended. For best results, read and follow the instructions listed on the container. For outdoor projects, use a waterproof glue such as *resorcinol* or *epoxy*.

If you plan to use stain for a finish, be sure the glue does not spread to areas other than those intended as this prevents proper absorption of the color into the wood.

Countersinking and Counterboring

The instructions for some of the projects call for countersinking flathead screws or counterboring holes so a dowel plug can be used to conceal the screw head. Examples of each type are shown below. Countersink and counterbore bits are available and fit most hand held drills.

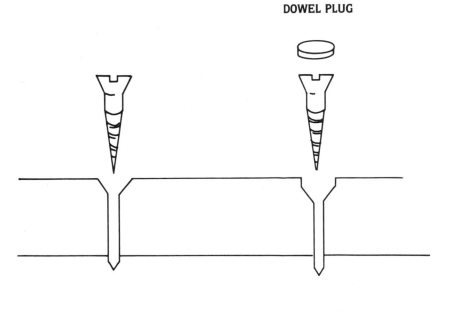

DOWEL PLUG

COUNTERSINK   COUNTERBORE

Enlarging a Pattern

To enlarge a pattern, create a grid on a piece of paper using the size squares called for in the instructions (example: 2″ squares). Make dots where the design crosses the grid lines on the original pattern. Draw corresponding dots on the larger grid pattern. Connect the dots. In busy areas, you may wish to increase the number of dots by increasing the reference lines. In these areas make an **X** in the square and add the additional dots.

To transfer a pattern directly to the board, place a piece of carbon paper between the drawing and the lumber and trace over the lines with a pencil. Use enough force to leave an impression on the wood beneath.

For a more durable pattern, make a cardboard template. To do this, just trace the pattern onto a piece of medium-weight cardboard and cut it out. This cut-out shape will allow you to quickly draw around the outside edge to reproduce the design as many times as you wish.

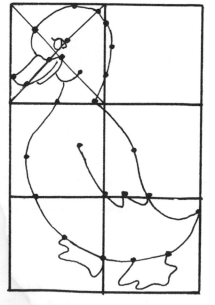
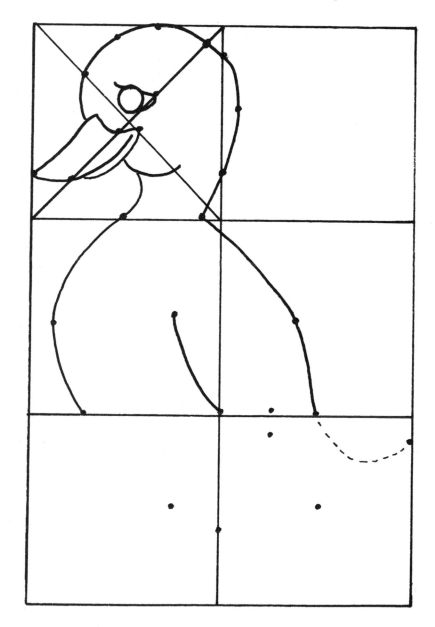

WALL HANGINGS

WELCOME

Welcome Plaque

12

1/2″ TO 3/4″ STOCK
SCALE: 1 SQUARE = 2″

Welcome Heart

1/2" TO 3/4" STOCK
SCALE: 1 SQUARE = 2"

13

Welcome Goose

Use 1/2" or 3/4" stock to make your welcome goose. Add a big bow at the neck and hang at the front door.

1/2" TO 3/4" STOCK
SCALE: 1 SQUARE = 2"

14

Welcome Bouquet

For your spring bouquet welcome plaque, cut the flowers and leaves from 1/4 to 3/4" stock using the pattern on page 16 and the welcome sign below. Assemble, as shown, using dowels for stems. Arrange five 1-1/4" lattice strips to create a picket fence. Attach the flowers and welcome sign to the fence using nails and/or glue.

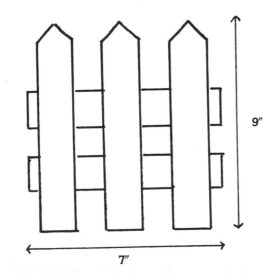

9"

7"

Spring Bouquet

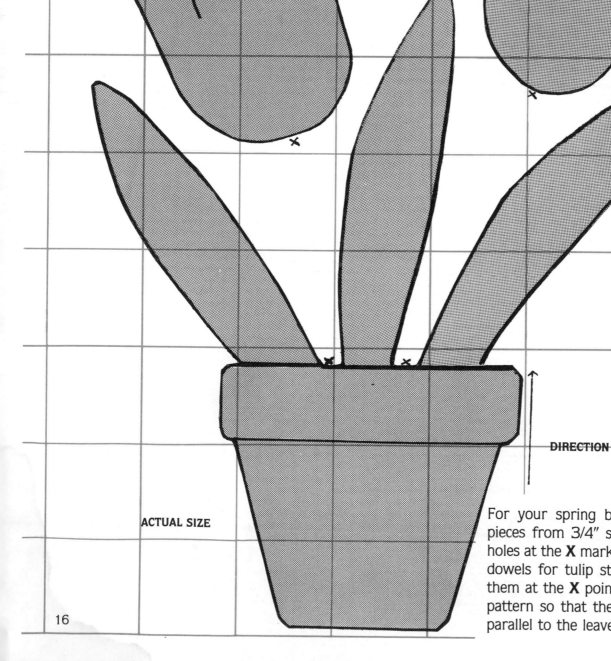

ACTUAL SIZE

DIRECTION OF GRAIN

For your spring bouquet, cut all pieces from 3/4" stock. Drill 1/4" holes at the **X** marks. Cut two 1/4" dowels for tulip stems and insert them at the **X** points. Position the pattern so that the wood grain is parallel to the leaves.

Kitchen Maid

Personalize this little cook by adding a name along the skirt hem and an apostrophe S. Trace the design the same size or enlarge it to 13" tall by making each square equal 2". Cut from 1/4" to 3/4" stock.

ABCDEFGHIJKLM'
NOPQRSTUVWXYZ

KITCHEN

Personalized Sign

Use the alphabet on page 17 to create a per-sonalized sign for your child's room. Cut the pattern the same size as shown, from 3/4" stock. Delete the bow and curls for a boy's room.

3/4" STOCK
ACTUAL SIZE

Kitchen Hang Ups

1/8" TO 3/4" STOCK
SHOWN ACTUAL SIZE

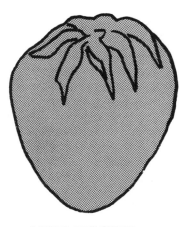

1/8" TO 3/4" STOCK
SHOWN ACTUAL SIZE

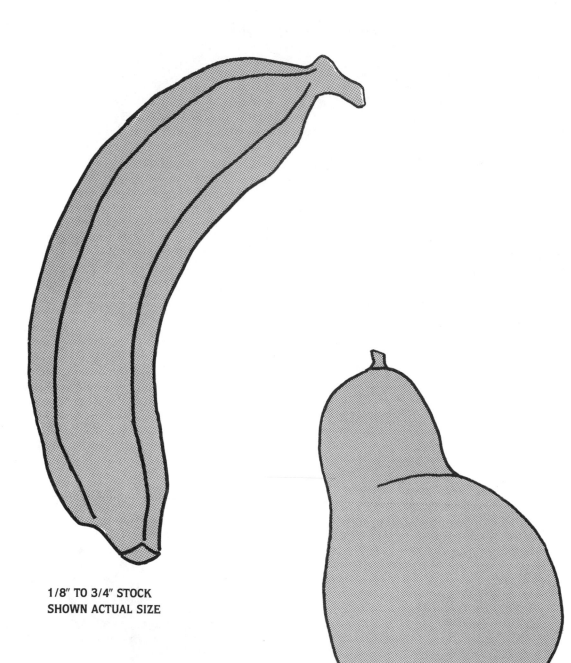

**1/8″ TO 3/4″ STOCK
SHOWN ACTUAL SIZE**

**1/8″ TO 3/4″ STOCK
SHOWN ACTUAL SIZE**

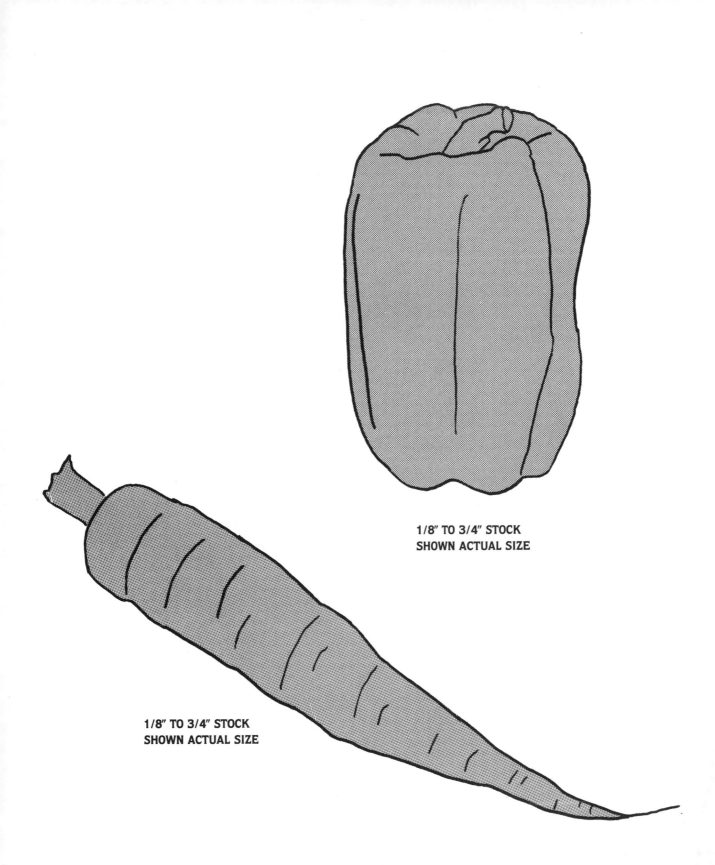

**1/8″ TO 3/4″ STOCK
SHOWN ACTUAL SIZE**

**1/8″ TO 3/4″ STOCK
SHOWN ACTUAL SIZE**

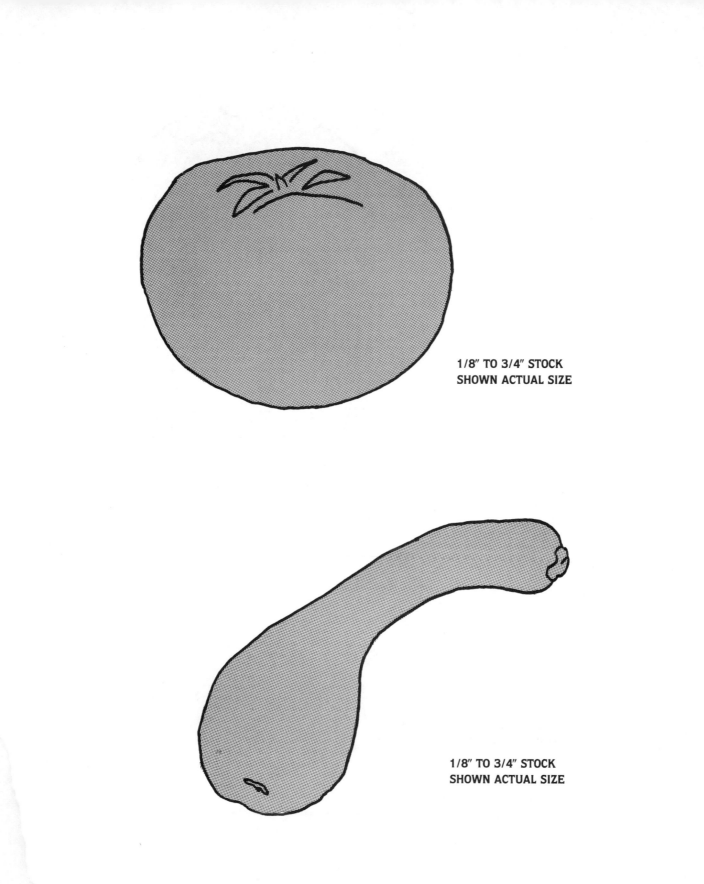

1/8″ TO 3/4″ STOCK
SHOWN ACTUAL SIZE

1/8″ TO 3/4″ STOCK
SHOWN ACTUAL SIZE

Baby Animals

These baby animals will decorate a shelf or brighten a windowsill. Cut them from 3/4″ stock following the broken lines for their bases. For a baby's room, enlarge the animals and cut the shapes from 1/8″ or 1/4″ plywood, omitting the base.

**3/4″ STOCK
ACTUAL SIZE**

Pig Family

Cut the little pig family from 3/4″ stock, following the dotted lines for the bases. You may wish to attach the figures to a 4″ × 12″ board.

For a nursery wall hanging, enlarge the animals and cut them from 1/8″ or 1/4″ plywood, omitting the base.

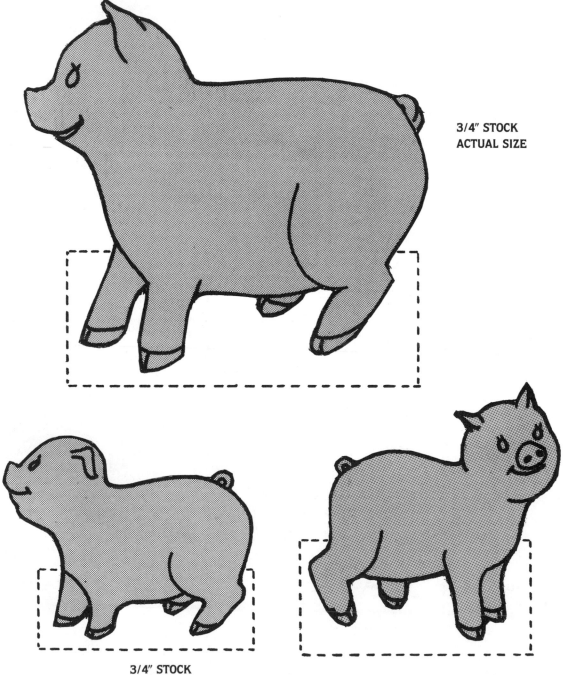

**3/4″ STOCK
ACTUAL SIZE**

**3/4″ STOCK
ACTUAL SIZE**

USEFUL ACCESSORIES

Novelty Baskets

Choose a novelty shape from the next three pages and cut two end pieces the same size as pictured. Drill a 3/8" hole at each **X** mark shown in the figure. Space nine 3/4" × 10" lattice strips around the outer edge of the shapes to create a basket, with three strips at the bottom. Cut a 10" length of 3/8" dowel and insert in the holes drilled to form a handle. Use small nails and glue to attach it to the sides.

Diagram for Teddy, Pineapple, and Bunny Baskets

Teddy Basket

3/4" STOCK
ACTUAL SIZE

Pineapple Basket

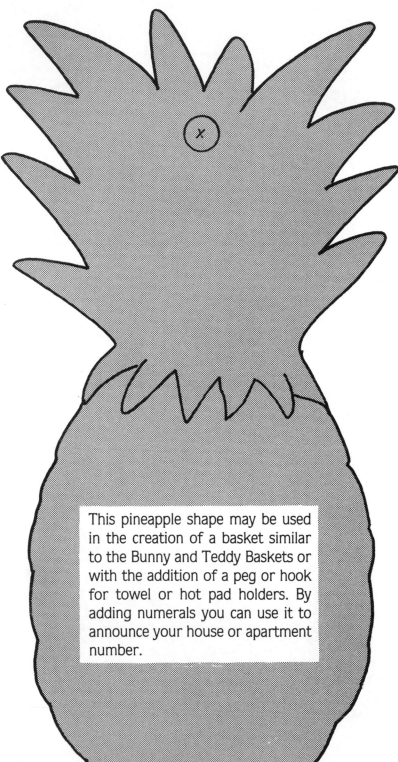

This pineapple shape may be used in the creation of a basket similar to the Bunny and Teddy Baskets or with the addition of a peg or hook for towel or hot pad holders. By adding numerals you can use it to announce your house or apartment number.

**3/4" STOCK
ACTUAL SIZE**

Bunny Basket

**3/4" STOCK
ACTUAL SIZE**

29

Chicken-Duck Baskets

Diagram for Chicken and Duck Baskets

Cut two animal shapes from 3/4" lumber the same size as the pattern pictured. Drill a 3/8" hole at the **X** mark in each handle brace. Space nine 3/4" × 10" lattice strips around the outer edge of the animal shapes to create a basket, with three strips at the bottom as shown in the diagram. Cut a 10" length of 3/8" dowel and insert it in the holes in the handle braces.

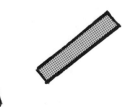

Chicken Basket

3/4″ STOCK
ACTUAL SIZE

Duck Basket

**3/4" STOCK
ACTUAL SIZE**

Carryall

Make a variety of these handy carryalls by changing dimensions

SMALL CARRYALL

1/2″ TO 3/4″ STOCK
SCALE: 1 SQUARE = 2″

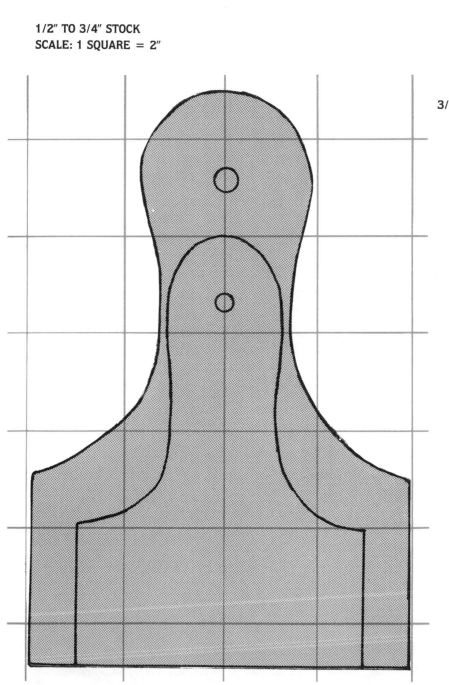

9″

3/8″ dia.

9″

3″

7-1/2″

6″

SMALL SIZE:
BOTTOM: 4-1/2″ × 7-1/2″
DOWEL: 3/8″ × 9″
ENDS: 6″ × 9″
SIDES: 3″ × 7-1/2″

LARGE CARRYALL

BOTTOM: 6-1/2″ × 10-1/2″
DOWEL: 1/2″ × 12″
ENDS: 8″ × 12″
SIDES: 4″ × 10-1/2″

Novelty Bookends or Plantholder

For either the bookends or plant holder, begin by cutting all pieces from 3/4″ stock. Position the body piece flat and attach the head in an upright manner at right angles. (The fit should be snug). Slip the tail piece in the slot, and secure by using glue and either nails or screws.

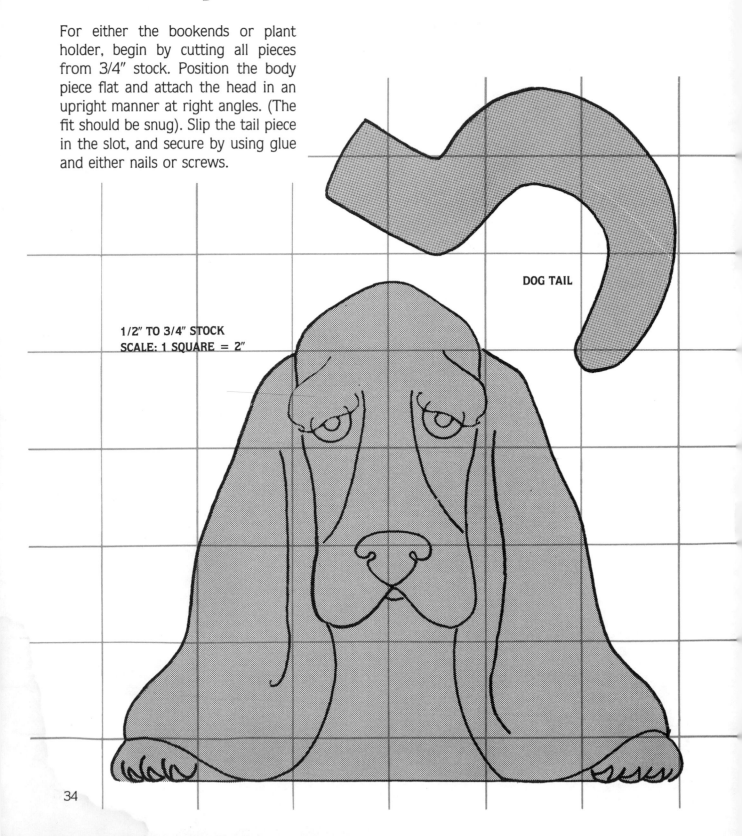

DOG TAIL

1/2″ TO 3/4″ STOCK
SCALE: 1 SQUARE = 2″

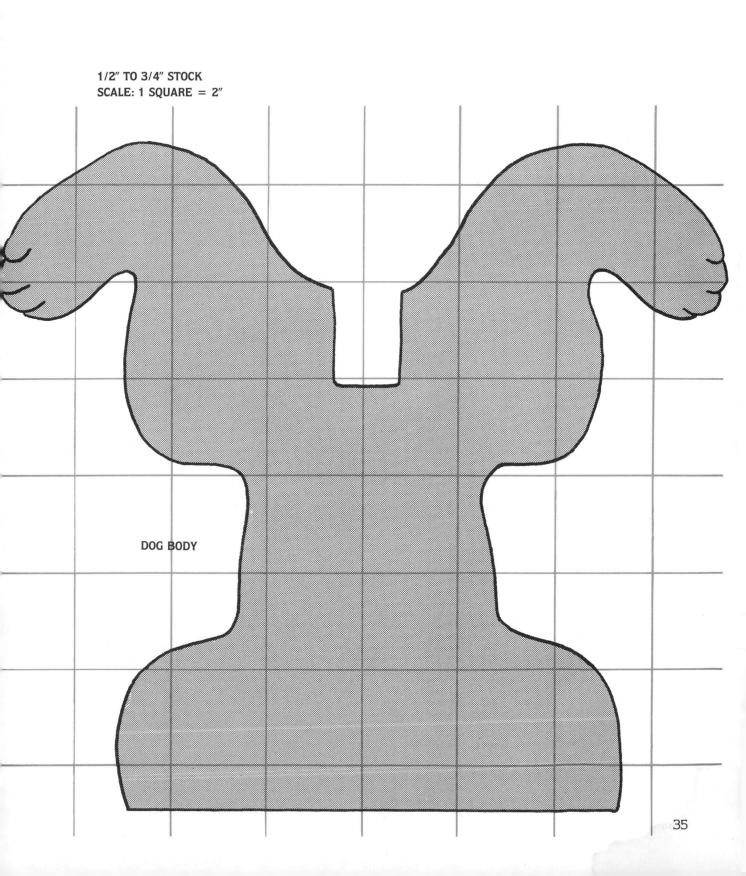

1/2″ TO 3/4″ STOCK
SCALE: 1 SQUARE = 2″

DOG BODY

35

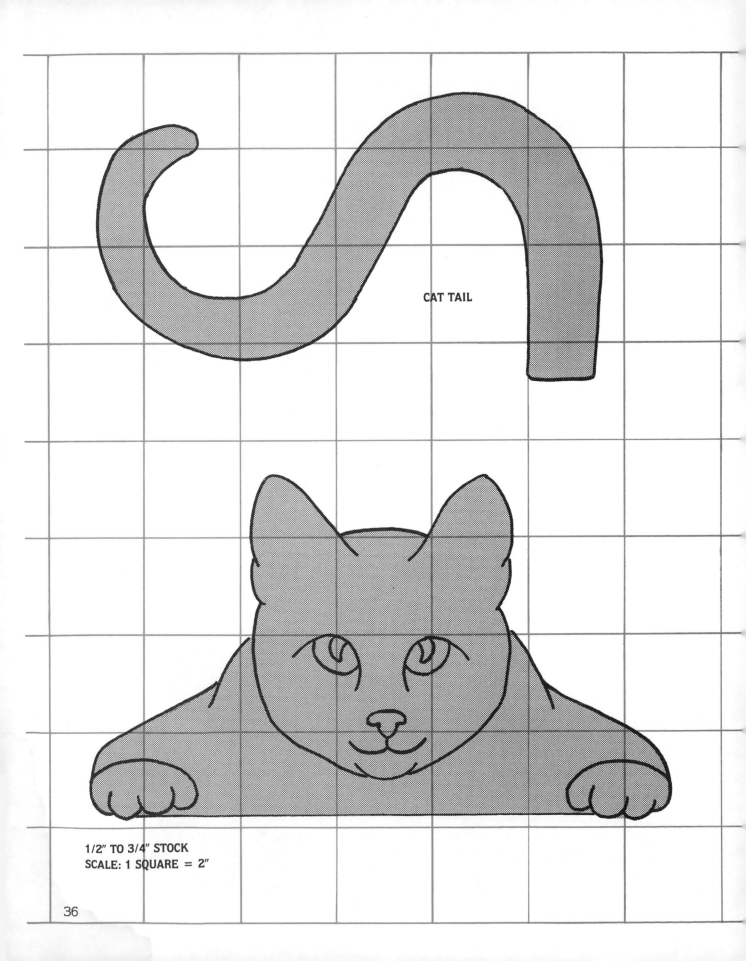

CAT TAIL

1/2" TO 3/4" STOCK
SCALE: 1 SQUARE = 2"

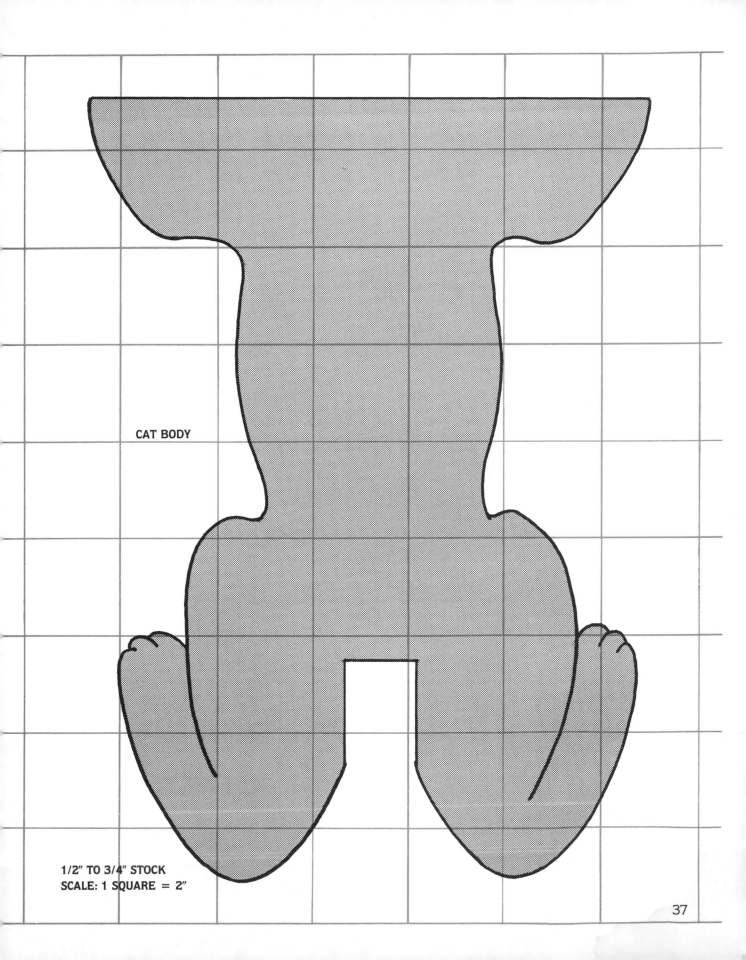

CAT BODY

1/2" TO 3/4" STOCK
SCALE: 1 SQUARE = 2"

37

Adjustable Bookends

Use the teapot design on the next page or the 7" squares to form one end and the movable support. Cut the left end, movable support and the right end, using 3/4" lumber. Drill holes as shown and cut two 1/2" dowels to the desired length. Fasten dowels in the end piece by gluing or nailing from the bottom side of the end pieces.

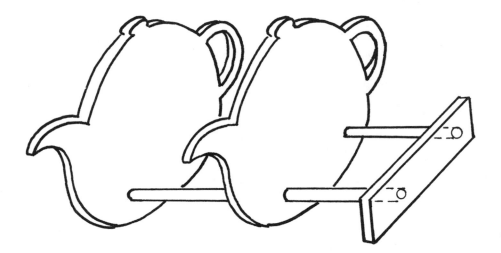

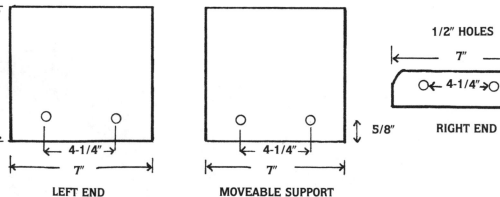

1/2" HOLES

9/16" HOLES

7"

4-1/4"

7"

LEFT END

4-1/4"

7"

5/8"

MOVEABLE SUPPORT

1/2" HOLES

7"

4-1/4"

1-1/2"

RIGHT END

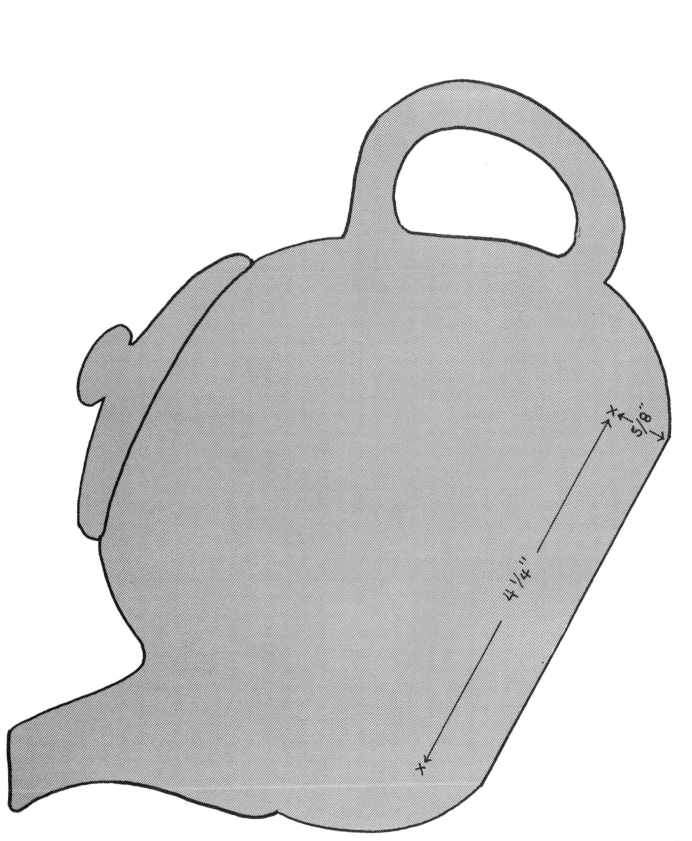

4¼"

⅝"

3/4" STOCK
ACTUAL SIZE

Adjustable Book Rack

This book rack design will be 16-1/2″ long, 10″ high and 8-3/4″ deep. You may wish to vary the dimensions in order to have it larger or smaller than shown.

Drill 9/16″ holes through the bottom as shown. The number of hole pairs depends on the usage. Drill 1/2″ holes 1″ deep in the movable separator and insert 1/2″ × 2″ dowels. Counterbore four holes in each end to receive 1-1/4″ No. 8 flathead screws and dowel plugs. The two holes at the bottom of each end should be centered 7/8″ from the lower edge.

Fasten the ends to the bottom and back. Using nails, fasten the back to the bottom.

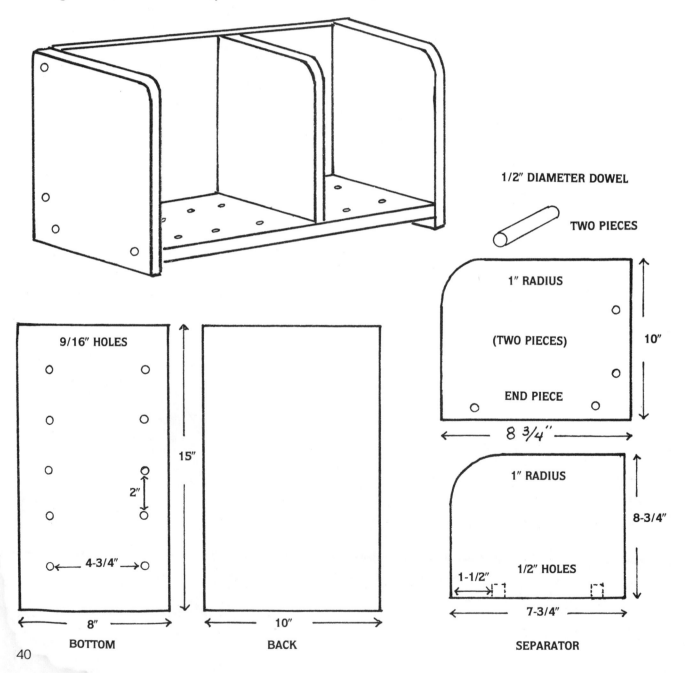

1/2″ DIAMETER DOWEL

TWO PIECES

1″ RADIUS

(TWO PIECES)

END PIECE

10″

8 3/4″

9/16″ HOLES

15″

2″

4-3/4″

8″

BOTTOM

BACK

10″

1″ RADIUS

8-3/4″

1/2″ HOLES

1-1/2″

7-3/4″

SEPARATOR

Key Organizer

Use 1/4″ to 3/4″ lumber and either "L" or cup
screw hooks. Use a bead or quarter-round bit
in the router for edging.

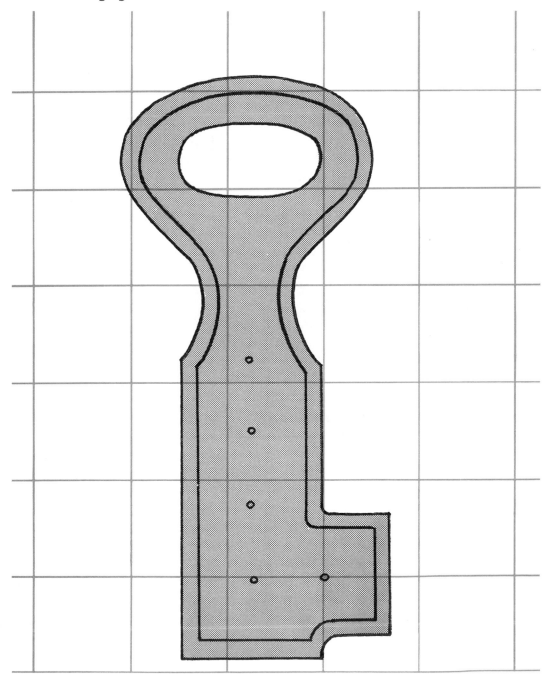

1/4″ TO 3/4″ STOCK
SCALE: 1 SQUARE = 2″

Key Organizer

Use 1/2″ or 3/4″ lumber and either "L" or cup
screw hooks.

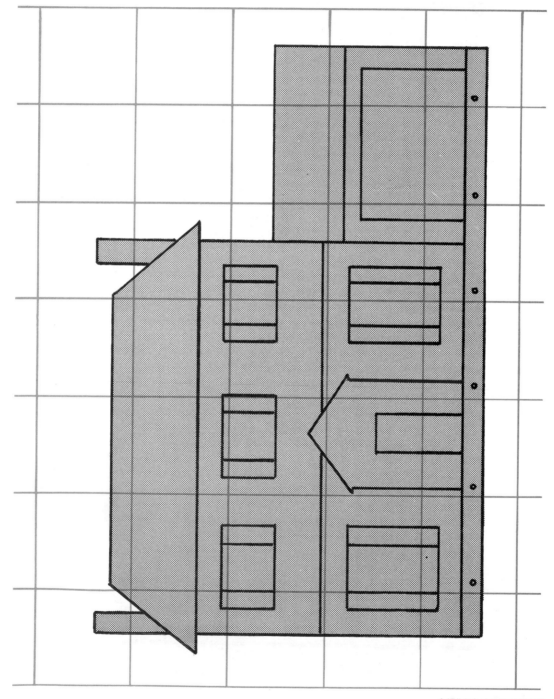

1/2″ TO 3/4″ STOCK
SCALE: 1 SQUARE = 2″

Key Organizer

Use 1/2″ or 3/4″ lumber and either "L" or cup
screw hooks.

**1/2″ TO 3/4″ STOCK
SCALE: 1 SQUARE = 2″**

Square Top Stool

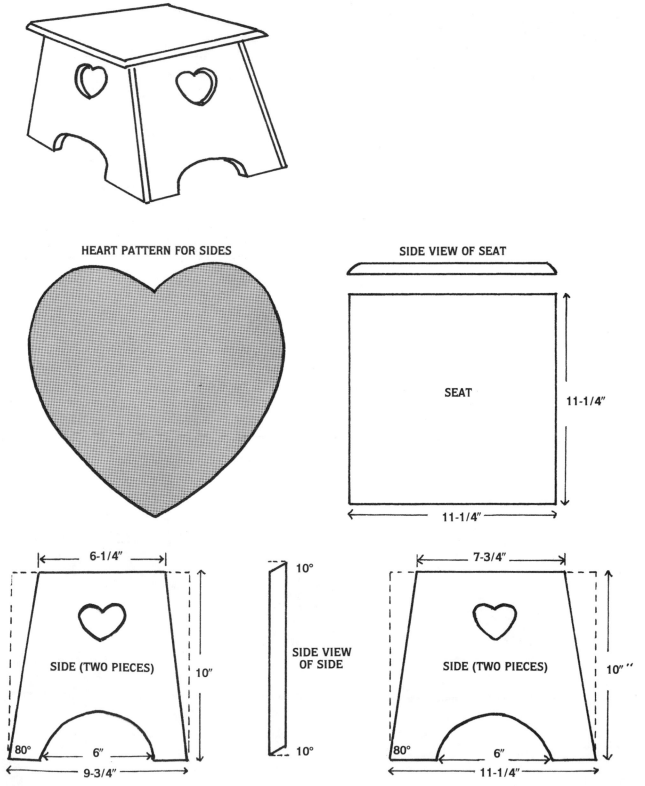

HEART PATTERN FOR SIDES

SIDE VIEW OF SEAT

SEAT

11-1/4″

11-1/4″

6-1/4″

SIDE (TWO PIECES)

10″

80°

6″

9-3/4″

10°

SIDE VIEW
OF SIDE

10°

7-3/4″

SIDE (TWO PIECES)

10″ ″

80°

6″

11-1/4″

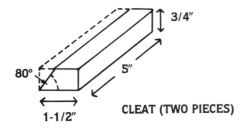

CLEAT (TWO PIECES)

3/4"

5"

80°

1-1/2"

Cut the seat piece and plane, rout or sand to round the top edges. Cut two sides 11-1/4" at the base and 7-3/4" at the top. Cut two sides 9-3/4" at the base and 6-1/4" at the top. Cut the heart shape in all four sides by first drilling a pilot hole, then completing the cut with a scroll saw, saber saw or coping saw.

For greater strength, use glue and screws at all joints. In the sides, counterbore holes as needed to receive #8 flathead screws and 3/8" dowel plugs. Using four 1-1/4" #8 flathead screws, attach the two cleats to the widest sides (top 7-3/4"), inset 1-3/8" from the edge. Attach the sides to each other as shown, using 1-1/4" #8 screws. Fill the holes with 3/8" dowel plugs. Drill pilot holes for screws in the cleats. Attach the seat to the sides using 1-1/4" #8 flathead screws.

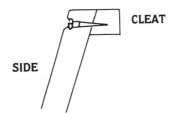

CLEAT

SIDE

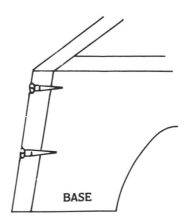

BASE

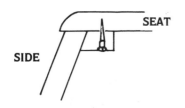

SEAT

SIDE

Oval Top Stool

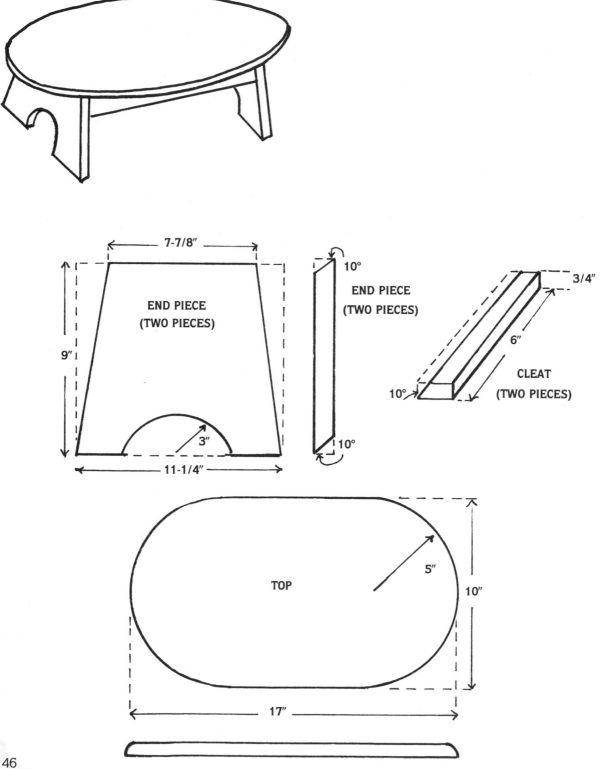

 END PIECE
(TWO PIECES)

7-7/8"

9"

11-1/4"

3"

10°

END PIECE
(TWO PIECES)

10°

3/4"

6"

10°

CLEAT
(TWO PIECES)

TOP

5"

10"

17"

Counterbore holes in the side and end pieces to receive screws and 3/8" dowel plugs. Glue all joints. Use 1−1/4" #8 flathead screws. Attach the two cleats to the two side supports, inset 15/16" from each edge. Attach two ends to two 2" side supports. Attach the seat to the side support pieces as shown. Drill pilot holes for screws.

CLEAT

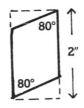

SIDE VIEW
SIDE SUPPORT

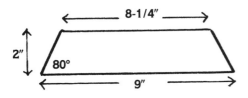

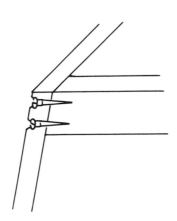

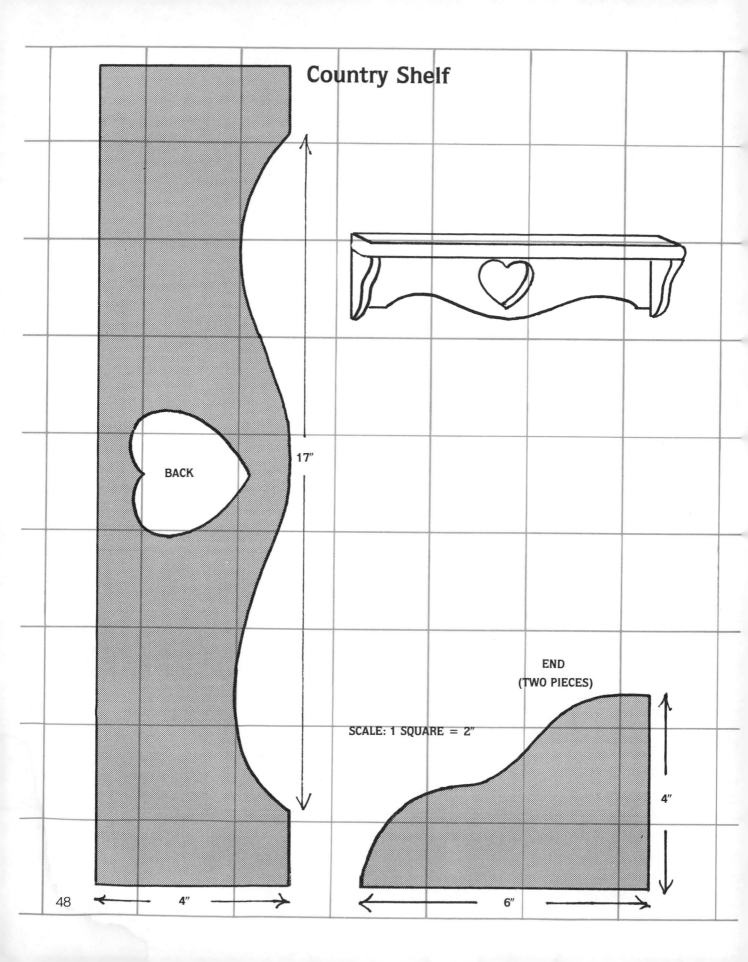

Country Shelf

BACK

17"

END
(TWO PIECES)

SCALE: 1 SQUARE = 2"

4"

4"

6"

48

This country shelf may be built in a variety of sizes by changing the dimensions. Be sure to consider the spacing of wall studs in your home; most older homes have studs spaced at 16″, and many of the newer homes use 24″ spacing.

Use 3/4″ stock. Cut the end pieces, back and top as shown. Edges should be rounded by using a router or by sanding. Find the center of the back piece and trace and cut out the heart shape by first drilling a pilot hole, then completing the cut. The shelf can be assembled by using nails or screws. If screws are used, counterbore holes to receive 1-1/4″ #8 flathead screws and 3/8″ dowel plugs.

HEART PATTERN

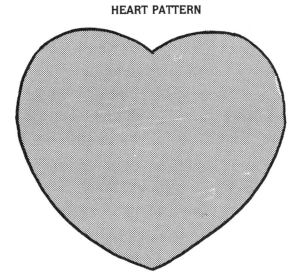

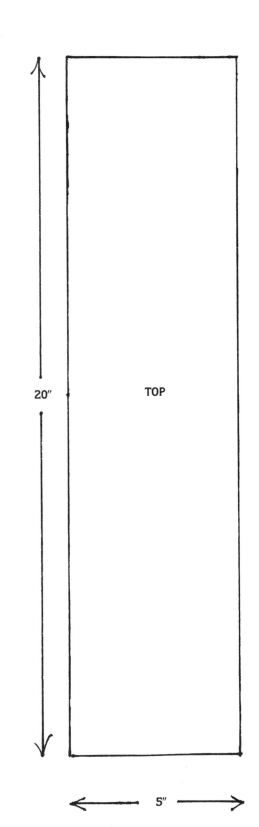

20″

TOP

5″

Granny Towel Rack

Cut your granny towel rack back from 3/4"
plywood, and use 3/4" lumber for the hands.
Drill a 1/2" hole in each hand piece. Assemble
the towel rack by using 1-1/4" #8 flathead
screws. (These should be countersunk.) Cut a
3/8" dowel 14-1/2" long to support the towels.
Use either a 3/4" or 1" diameter dowel for the
support ends. Cut two to the length of 3/4".
Drill 3/8" holes halfway through the dowel end
supports. Insert one end of the dowel into one
end support, using glue to bond it. Place the
dowel through the two holes cut in the hand
pieces and slip the second support end over the
end of the dowel. Do not glue.

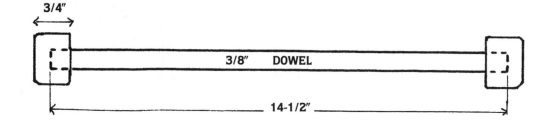

3/4"

3/8"   DOWEL

14-1/2"

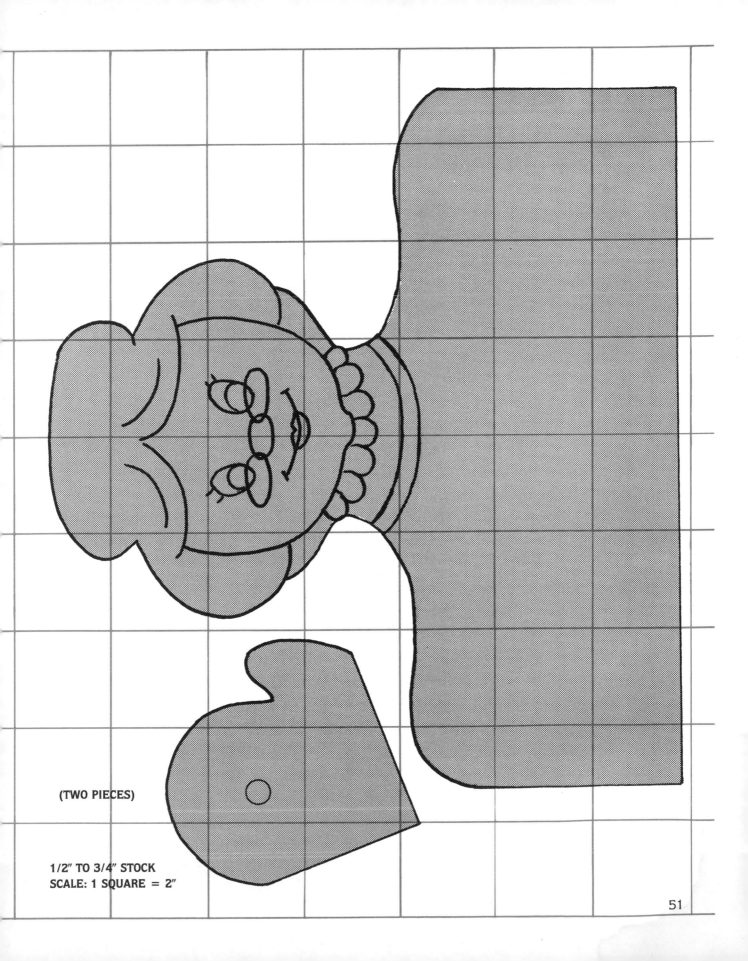

(TWO PIECES)

1/2" TO 3/4" STOCK
SCALE: 1 SQUARE = 2"

STAND-UP FIGURES

Little Bo-Peep

3/4" STOCK
ACTUAL SIZE

Cut one each of the girl and lamb figure. Cut
two arms and attach one to each side of the girl
at the **X**. Mount on a 4″ × 12″ board and tie
a ribbon from the girl's hand to the lamb's neck.

**3/4″ STOCK
ACTUAL SIZE**

Movable Teddy

Cut one teddy shape and two each of the arm and leg shapes of 3/4″ stock. Attach limbs to teddy at **X** points on each side by drilling 1/4″ holes and inserting 1/4″ dowels.

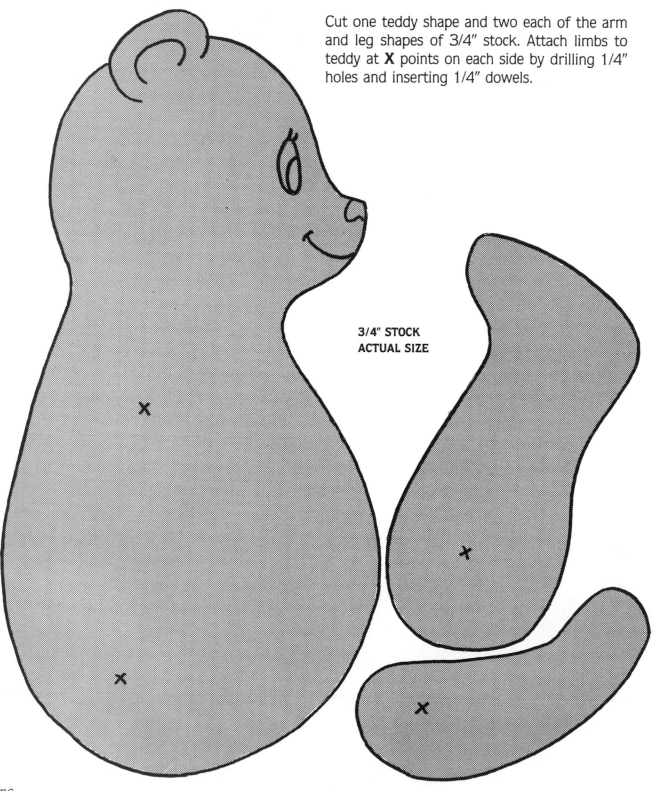

**3/4″ STOCK
ACTUAL SIZE**

Movable Mouse

Use 3/4″ stock to make your movable mouse. Cut one mouse shape and two arm shapes. Drill 1/4″ holes in the arms and the mouse shape at the **X** points. Attach the arms to each side by inserting a 1/4″ dowel.

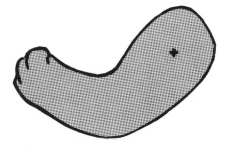

**3/4″ STOCK
ACTUAL SIZE**

Movable Bunny

To make a bunny with movable arms, cut one bunny shape and two arm shapes. Drill 1/4" holes in the arms and bunny at the **X** points. Attach the arms to each side by inserting a 1/4" dowel.

**3/4" STOCK
ACTUAL SIZE**

Garden Maid

Attach a stake to the back of the little maid and display in your garden or patio.

1/2″ TO 3/4″ STOCK
SCALE: 1 SQUARE = 2″

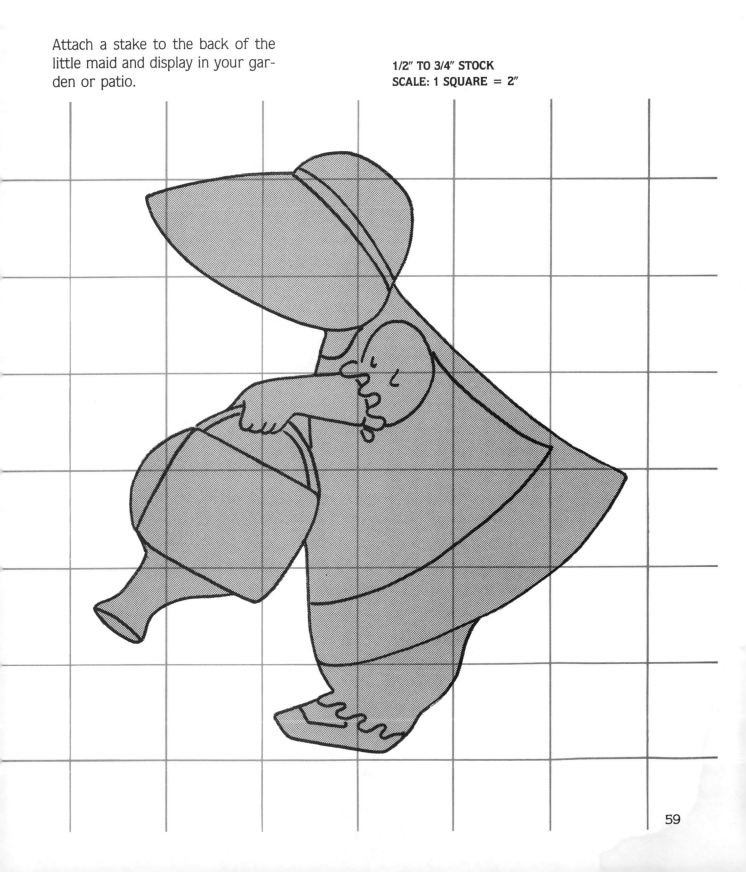

Rocking Horse

Cut one horse shape and two each of the leg-rocker shapes from 3/4" board. Attach a leg-rocker assembly to each side of the horse at the **X** point by drilling a 1/4" hole and inserting a 1/4" dowel.

**3/4" STOCK
ACTUAL SIZE**

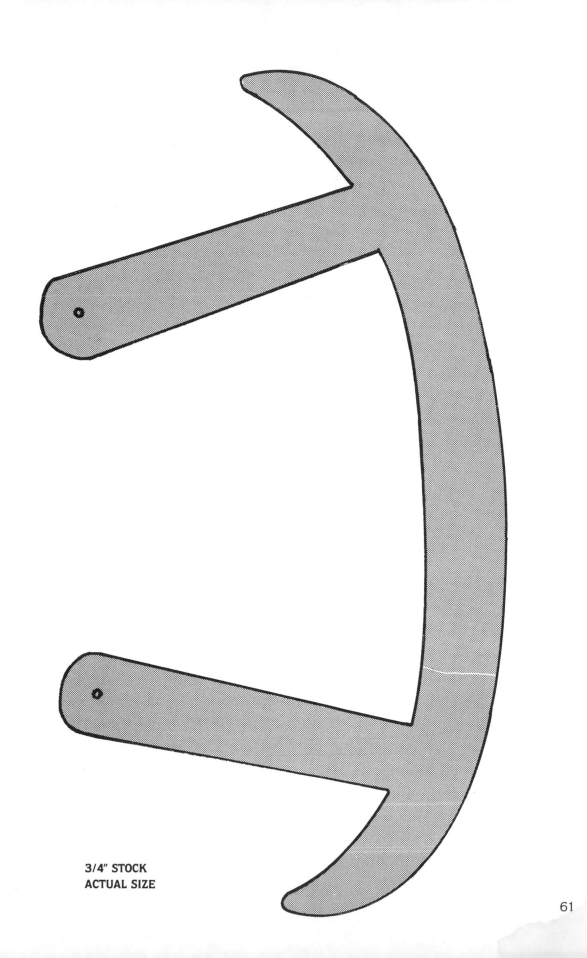

**3/4″ STOCK
ACTUAL SIZE**

61

Birth Announcer

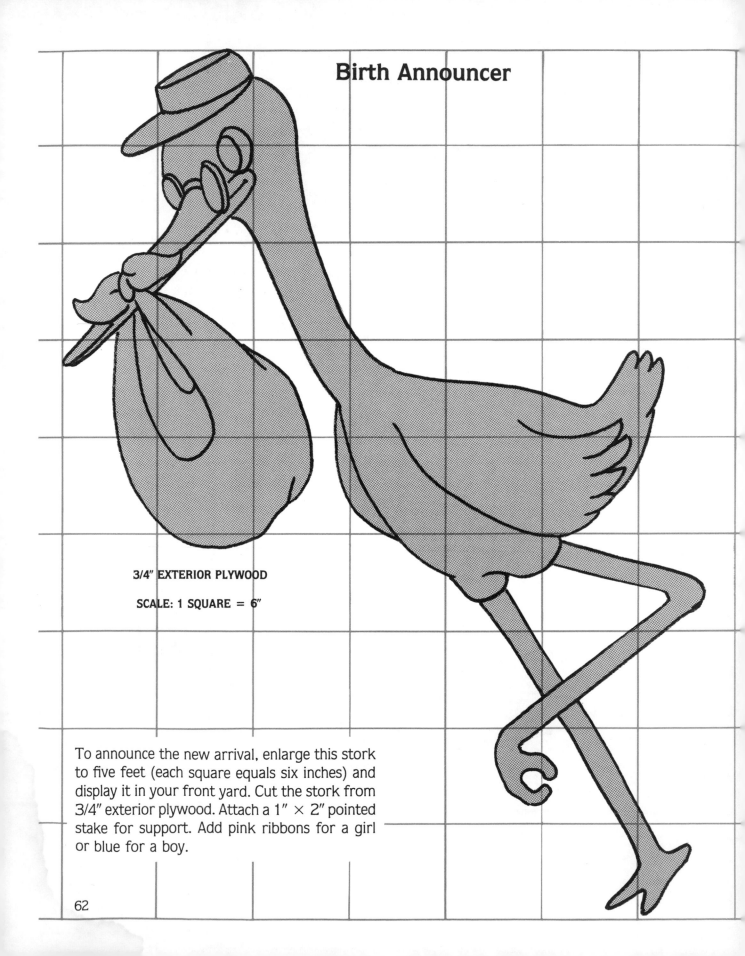

3/4" EXTERIOR PLYWOOD

SCALE: 1 SQUARE = 6"

To announce the new arrival, enlarge this stork to five feet (each square equals six inches) and display it in your front yard. Cut the stork from 3/4" exterior plywood. Attach a 1" × 2" pointed stake for support. Add pink ribbons for a girl or blue for a boy.

HOLIDAY DECORATIONS

Valentine Angel

1/2″ TO 3/4″ STOCK
SCALE: 1 SQUARE = 2″

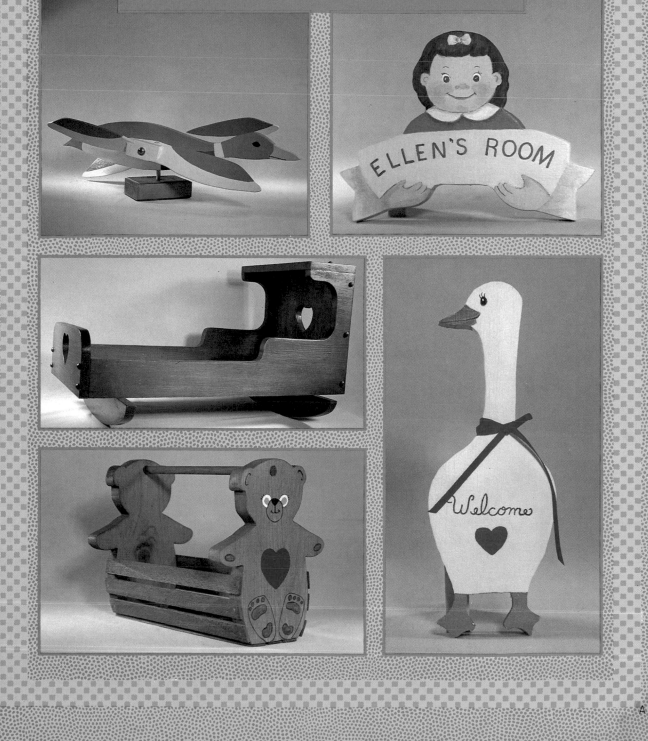

Clockwise from left: Whirling Bird (pp. 144–146); Personalized Sign (p. 18); Welcome Goose (p. 14); Teddy Basket (pp. 26, 27); Covered Top Cradle (pp. 122, 125).

ELLEN'S ROOM

Welcome

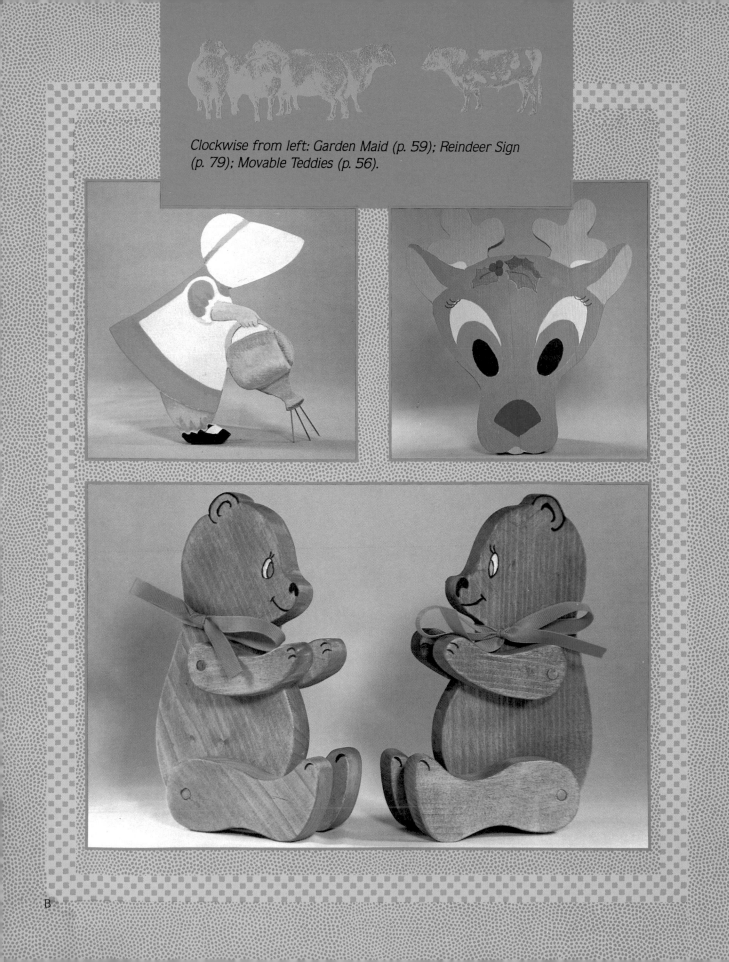

Clockwise from left: Garden Maid (p. 59); Reindeer Sign (p. 79); Movable Teddies (p. 56).

Clockwise from left: Valentine Angel (p. 64); Slant Roof Birdhouse (p. 141); Halloween Friends (p. 68); Clown (p. 99);
Thanksgiving Pilgrims (p. 70).

I LOVE YOU

C

Clockwise from left: Happy Snowman (p. 82); Kitchen Maid (p. 17); Easter Chick (p. 67); Rocking Horse (p. 60).

ANDREA'S

KITCHEN

HAPPY EASTER

Valentine Dragon

1/2″ TO 3/4″ STOCK
SCALE: 1 SQUARE = 2″

65

Easter Bunny

1/2" TO 3/4" STOCK
SCALE: 1 SQUARE = 2"

66

Easter Chick

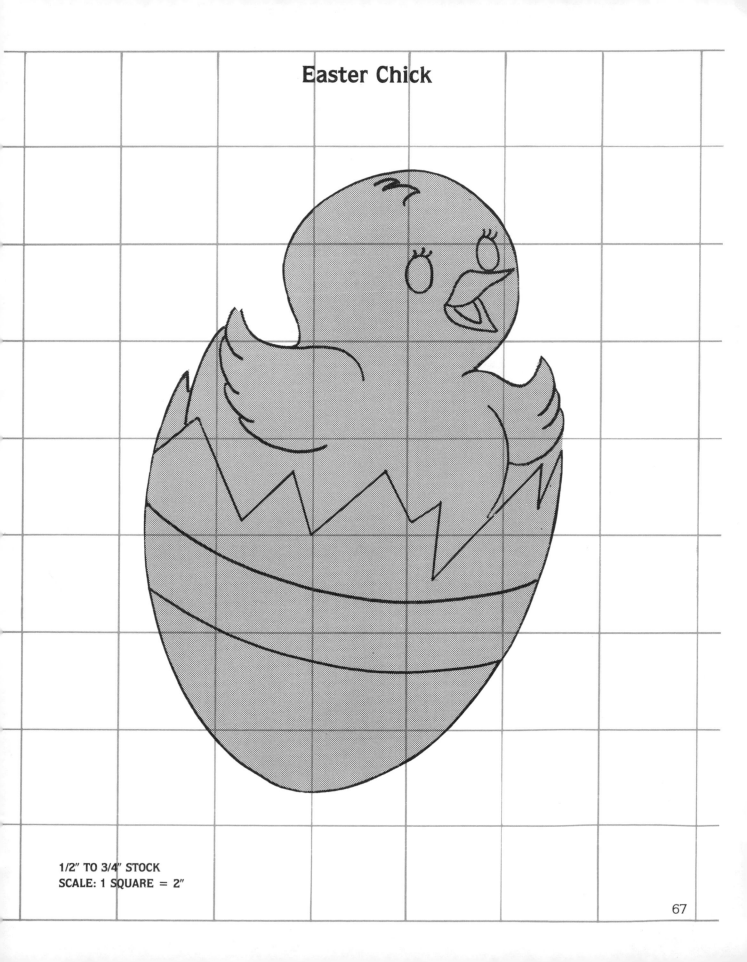

1/2" TO 3/4" STOCK
SCALE: 1 SQUARE = 2"

Halloween Friends

1/4″ TO 3/4″ PLYWOOD.

FOR WINDOW DECORATION: 1 SQUARE = 2″
FOR YARD DECORATION: 1 SQUARE = 6″

Little Spooks

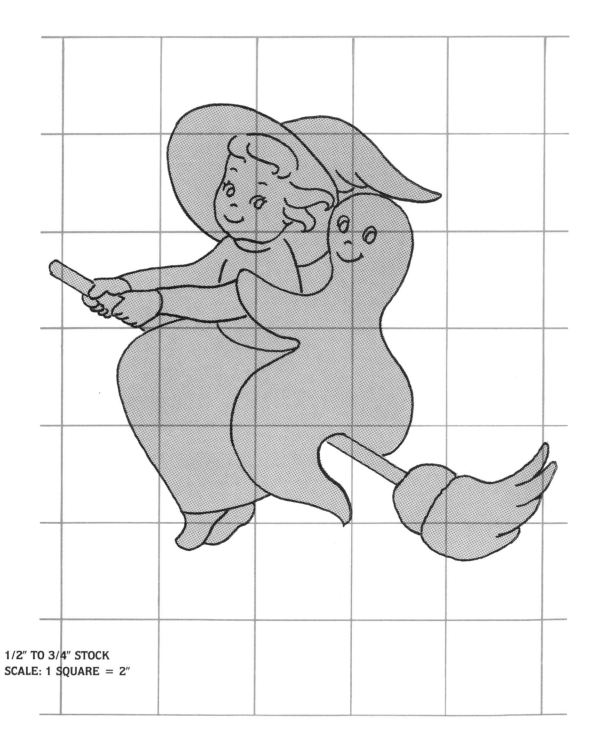

1/2″ TO 3/4″ STOCK
SCALE: 1 SQUARE = 2″

Thanksgiving Pilgrims

1/2" TO 3/4" STOCK
SCALE: 1 SQUARE = 2"

70

Thanksgiving Turkey

ADD YOUR OWN MESSAGE USING LETTERS ON PAGE 17.

1/2″ TO 3/4″ STOCK
SCALE: 1 SQUARE = 2″

Christmas Tree

Cut the two tree shapes from exterior plywood.
Cut one with the star on top and the slit half
way up from the bottom. Cut the other tree
shape without a star on top and the slit half
way down from the top. Slide the two together.
Finish with exterior paint.

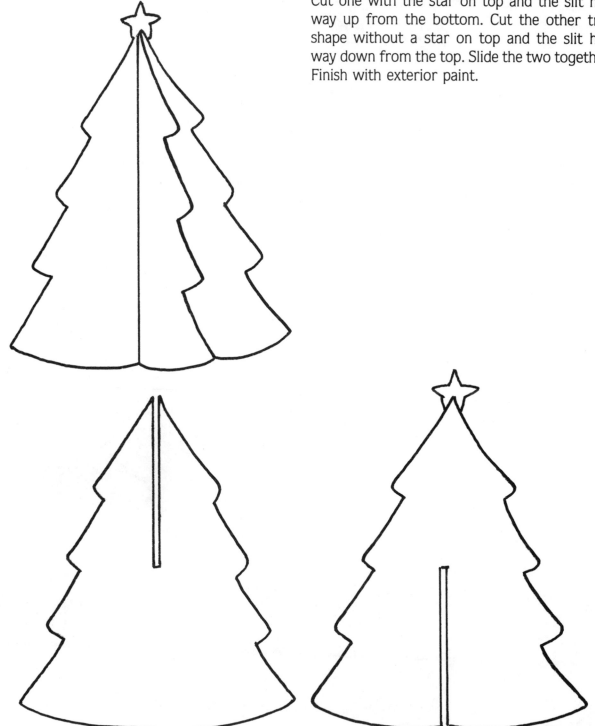

1/2″ TO 3/4″ EXTERIOR PLYWOOD   SCALE: 1 SQUARE = 6″

Nativity Scene

SCALE: 1 SQUARE = 6"

Use 1/2″ to 3/4″ outside plywood to make your nativity scene. Enlarge the designs to 6 times the size shown by making each square equal 6″. To display your Christmas decorations, mount a 1″ × 3″ brace across the back of the larger figures and attach 1″ × 3″ pointed stakes. For the smaller figures, a cross brace may not be needed. Extend the stakes up the back of the figure 2/3 of the height.

SCALE: 1 SQUARE = 6″

SCALE: 1 SQUARE = 6"

SCALE: 1 SQUARE = 6"

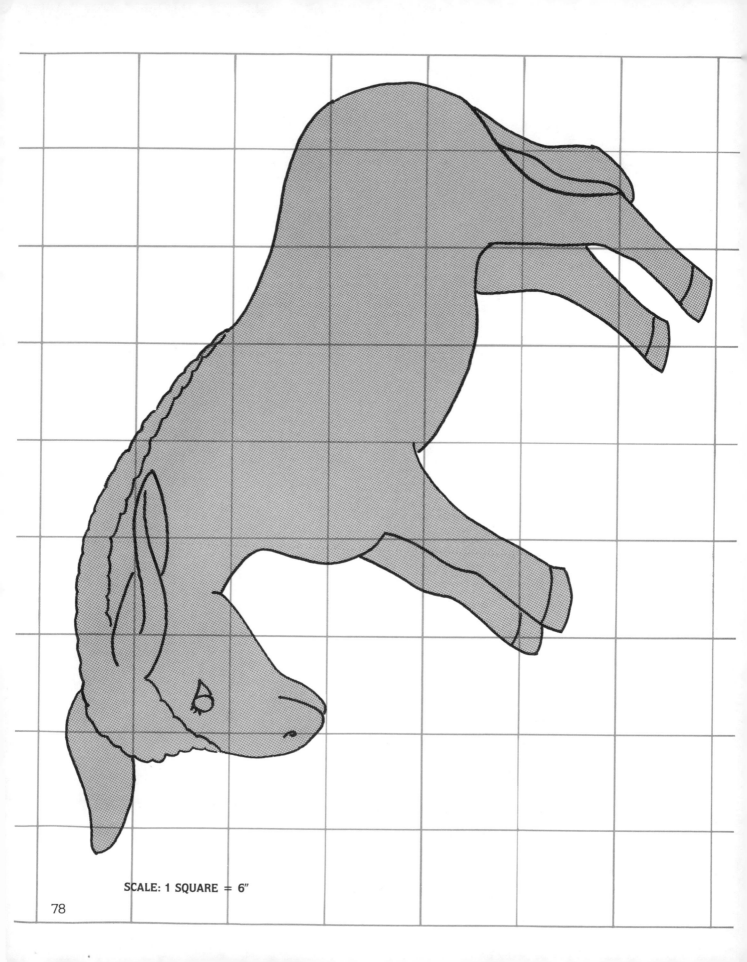

SCALE: 1 SQUARE = 6"

Reindeer Sign

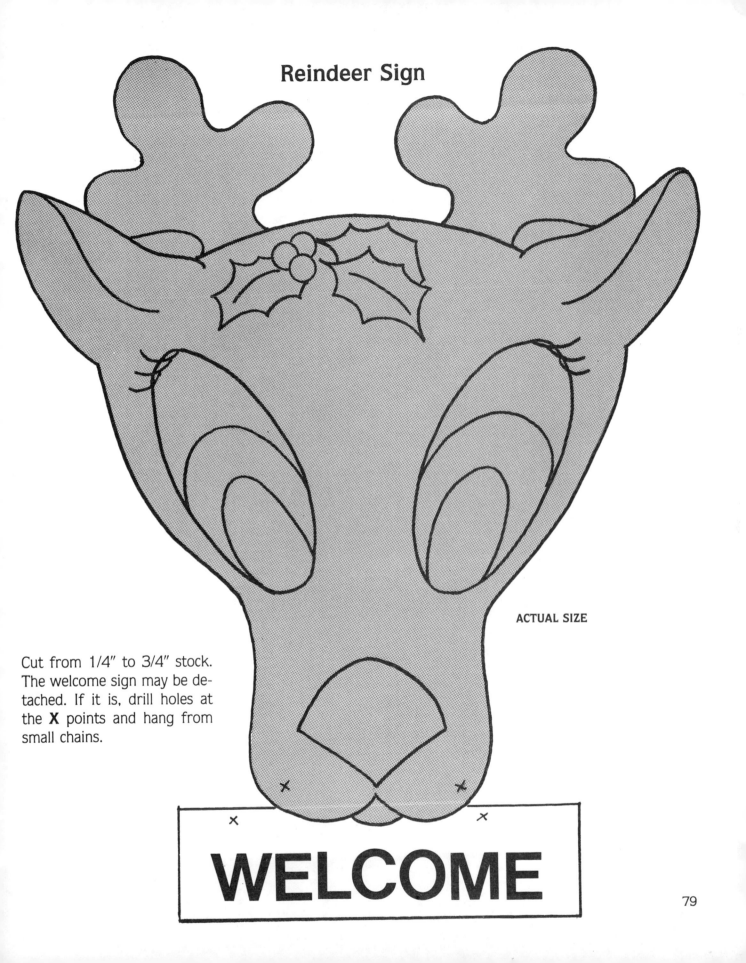

ACTUAL SIZE

Cut from 1/4″ to 3/4″ stock. The welcome sign may be detached. If it is, drill holes at the **X** points and hang from small chains.

WELCOME

Smiling Santa

1/2" TO 3/4" STOCK
SCALE: 1 SQUARE = 2"

80

Santa Figure

3/4" EXTERIOR PLYWOOD

SCALE: 1 SQUARE = 6"

81

Happy Snowman

For a 13″ snowman to hang on your front door or in a window, make each square equal 2″. Cut from 1/4″ plywood. To create a yard decoration, enlarge to 39″ by having each square equal 6″. Cut from 1/4″ or 3/4″ outside plywood.

SCALE: 1 SQUARE = 6″

Reindeer Basket

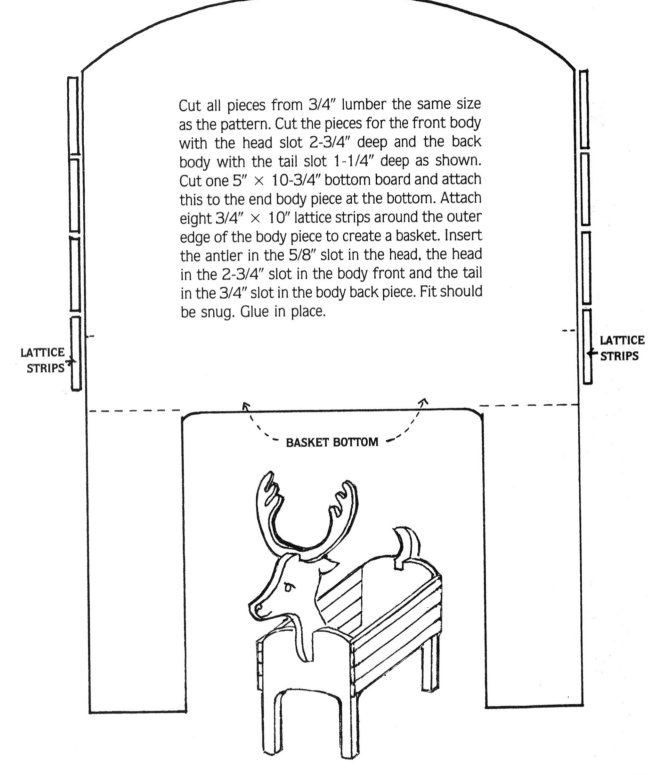

Cut all pieces from 3/4″ lumber the same size as the pattern. Cut the pieces for the front body with the head slot 2-3/4″ deep and the back body with the tail slot 1-1/4″ deep as shown. Cut one 5″ × 10-3/4″ bottom board and attach this to the end body piece at the bottom. Attach eight 3/4″ × 10″ lattice strips around the outer edge of the body piece to create a basket. Insert the antler in the 5/8″ slot in the head, the head in the 2-3/4″ slot in the body front and the tail in the 3/4″ slot in the body back piece. Fit should be snug. Glue in place.

LATTICE STRIPS

LATTICE STRIPS

BASKET BOTTOM

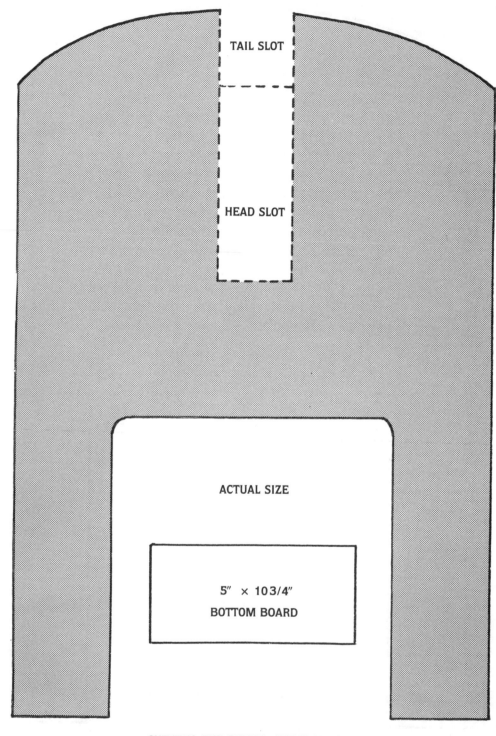

TAIL SLOT

HEAD SLOT

ACTUAL SIZE

5" × 103/4"
BOTTOM BOARD

CUT TWO END PIECES. CUT SLOT FOR
TAIL IN ONE. CUT SLOT FOR HEAD
IN THE OTHER.

84

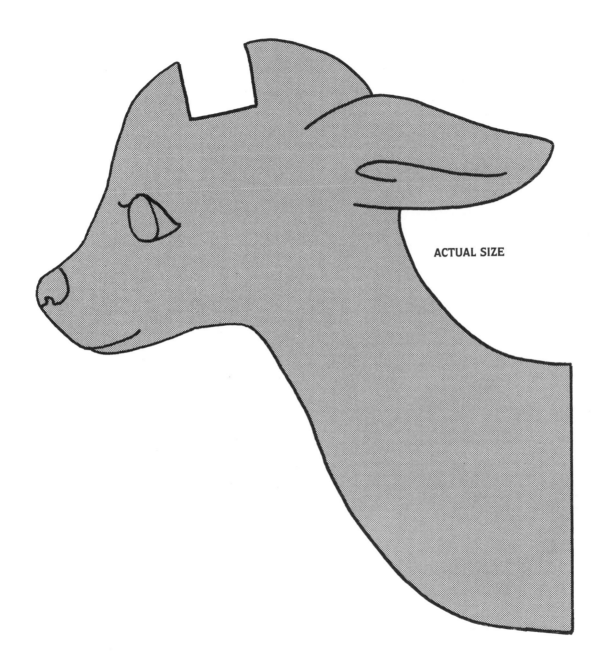

ACTUAL SIZE

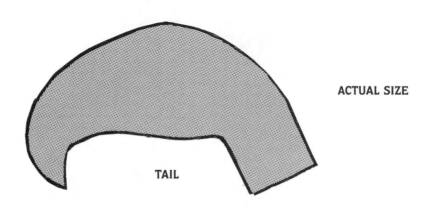

ACTUAL SIZE

TAIL

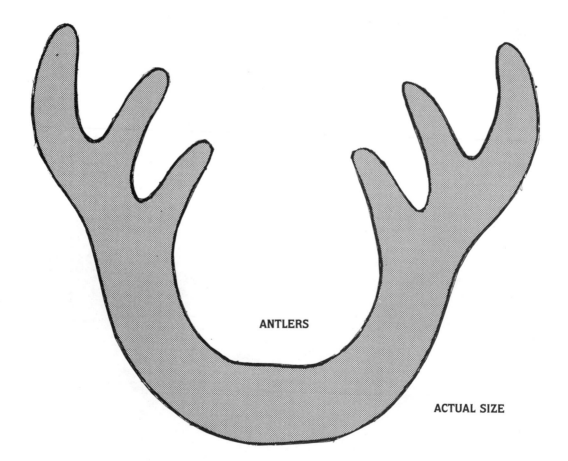

ANTLERS

ACTUAL SIZE

NURSERY WALL HANGINGS

Cat Family

1/8" TO 3/4" STOCK
1" OR 2" SQUARES

Ducklings

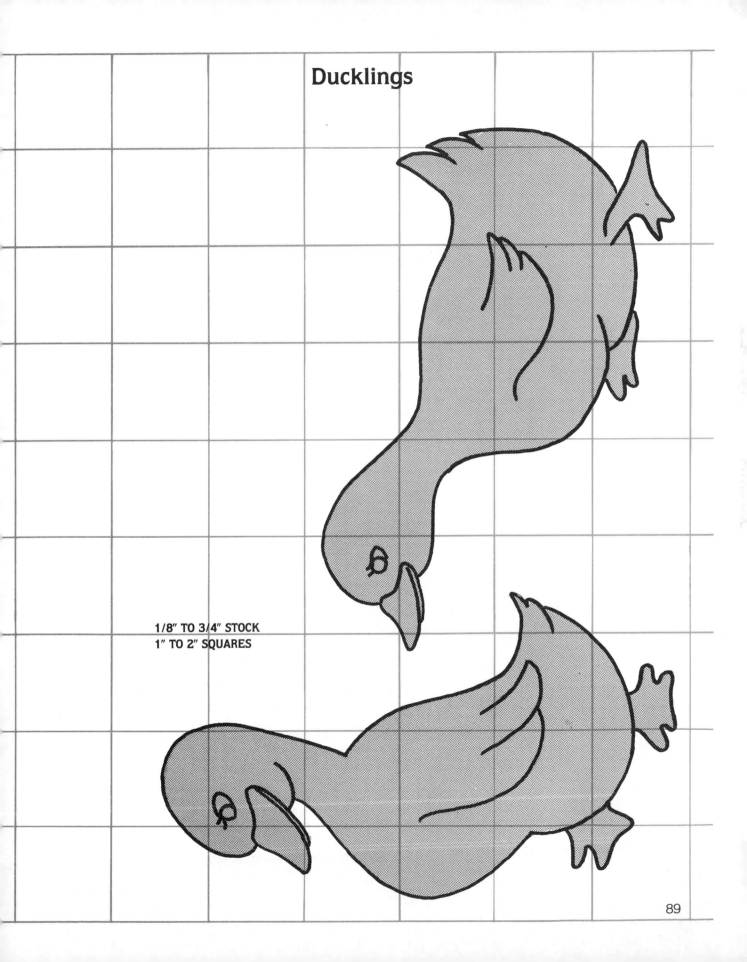

1/8" TO 3/4" STOCK
1" TO 2" SQUARES

89

1/8" TO 3/4" STOCK
1" TO 2" SQUARES

Honey Bear

1/8″ TO 3/4″ STOCK
1″ TO 2″ SQUARES

Monkey

1/8" TO 3/4" STOCK
1" OR 2" SQUARES

Basset Hound

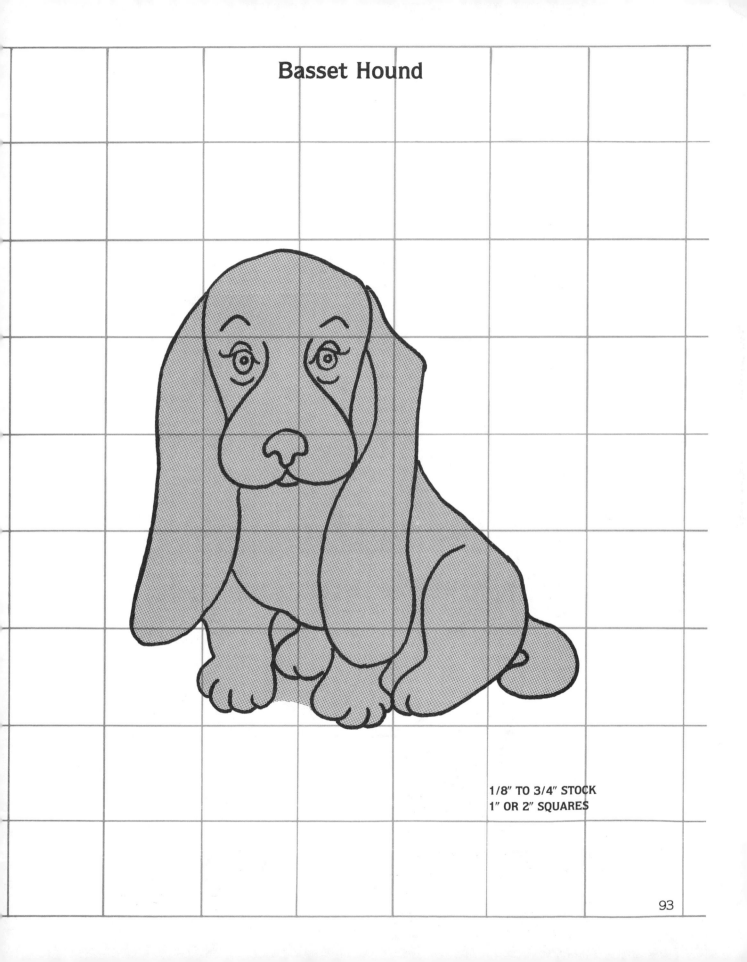

1/8″ TO 3/4″ STOCK
1″ OR 2″ SQUARES

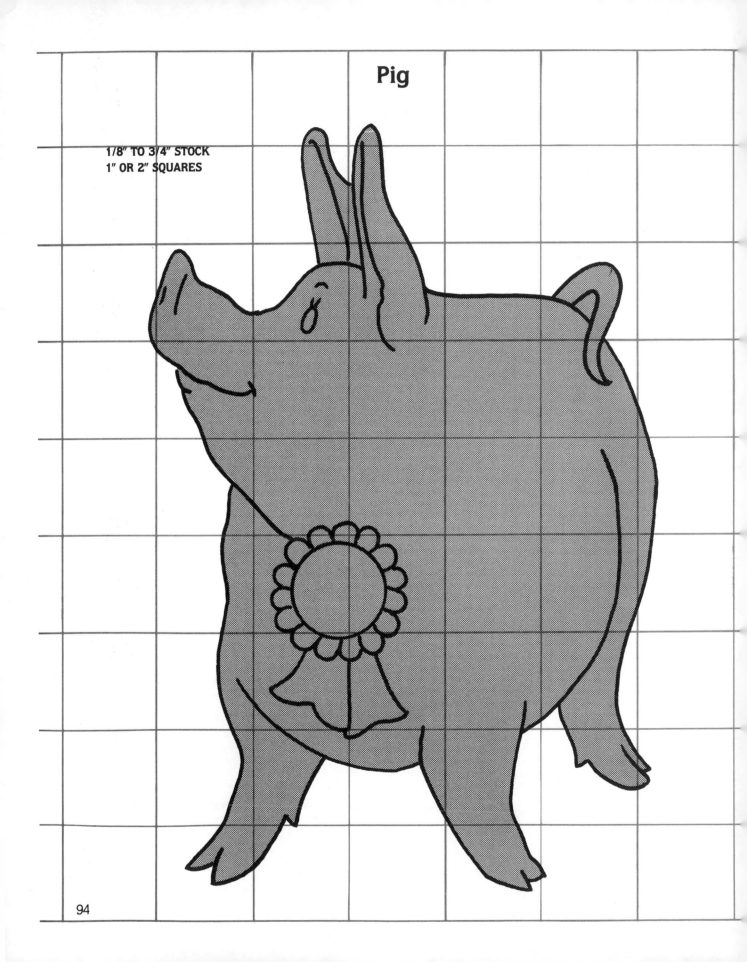

Pig

1/8" TO 3/4" STOCK
1" OR 2" SQUARES

Duck Family

1/8" TO 3/4" STOCK
1" TO 2" SQUARES

95

Farmer Boy

1/8″ TO 3/4″ STOCK
1″ OR 2″ SQUARES

Farmer Girl

1/8" TO 3/4" STOCK
1" OR 2" SQUARES

Little Miss Muffett

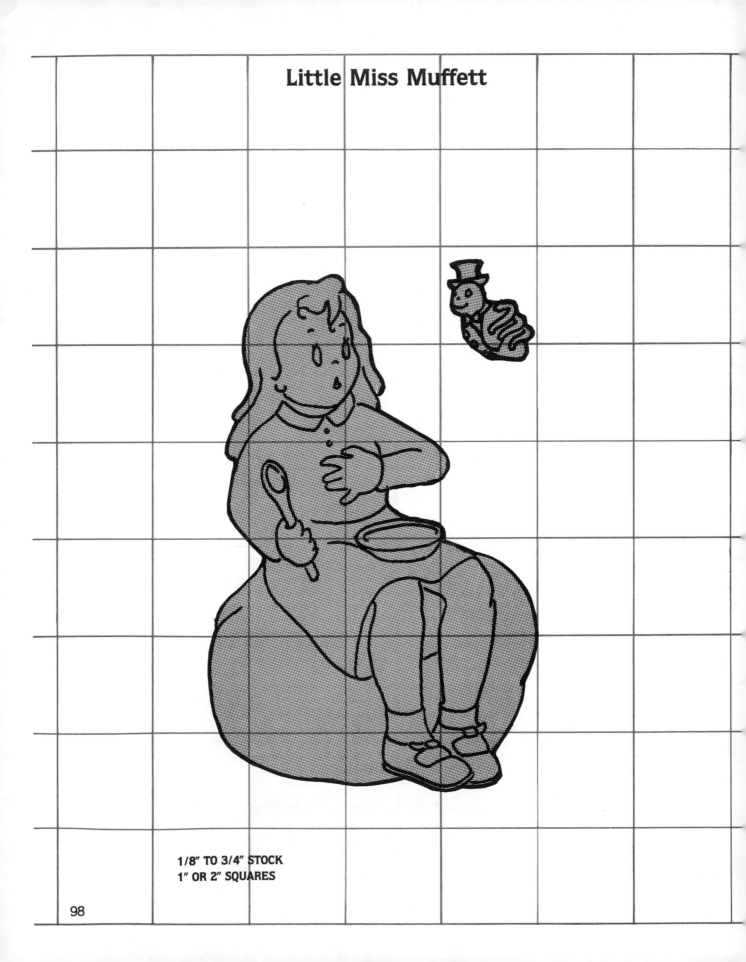

1/8" TO 3/4" STOCK
1" OR 2" SQUARES

Clown

1/8" TO 3/4" STOCK
1" OR 2" SQUARES

99

Toy Train

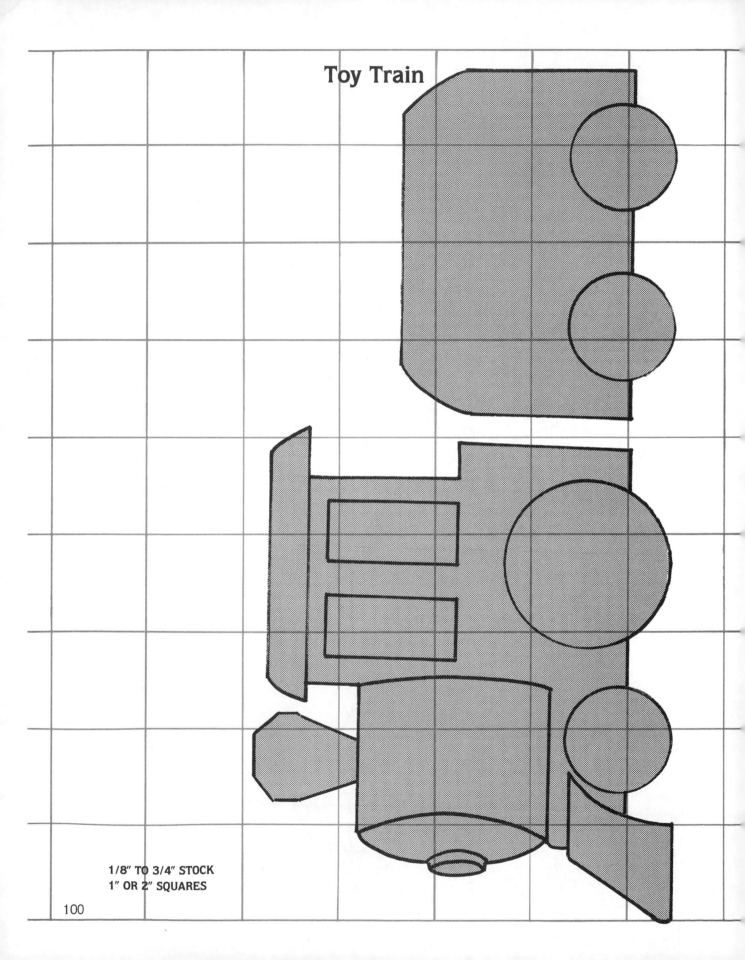

1/8" TO 3/4" STOCK
1" OR 2" SQUARES

100

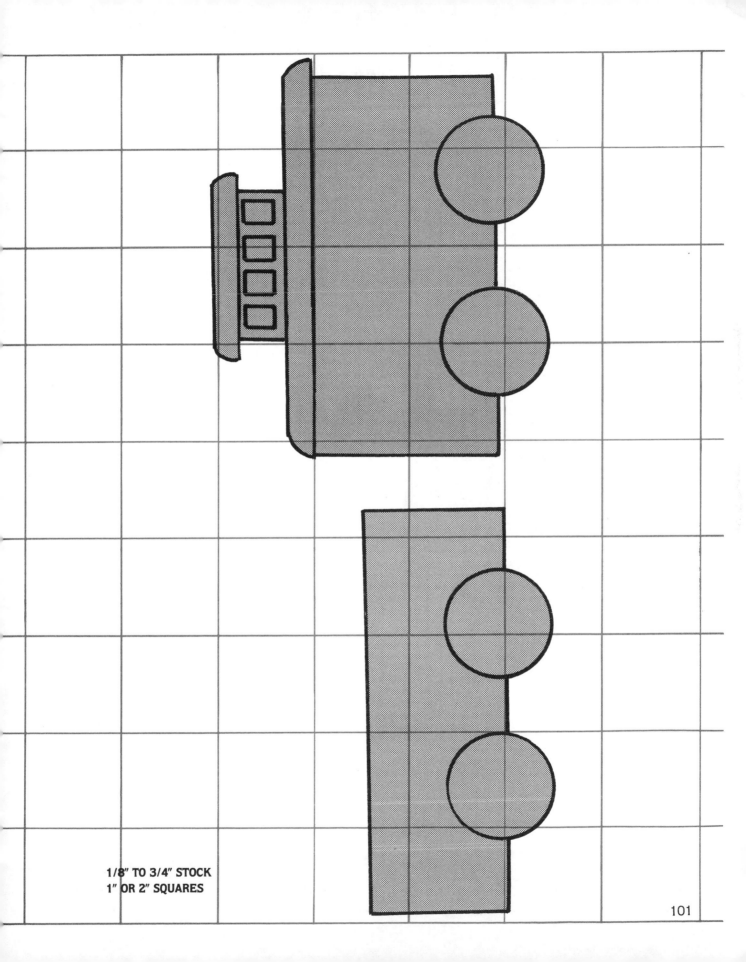

1/8" TO 3/4" STOCK
1" OR 2" SQUARES

101

Toy Soldiers

1/8" TO 3/4" STOCK
1" TO 2" SQUARES

102

1/8" TO 3/4" STOCK
1" TO 2" SQUARES

103

1/8″ TO 3/4″ STOCK
1″ TO 2″ SQUARES

104

1/8" TO 3/4" STOCK
1" OR 2" SQUARES

105

Little Boy Blue

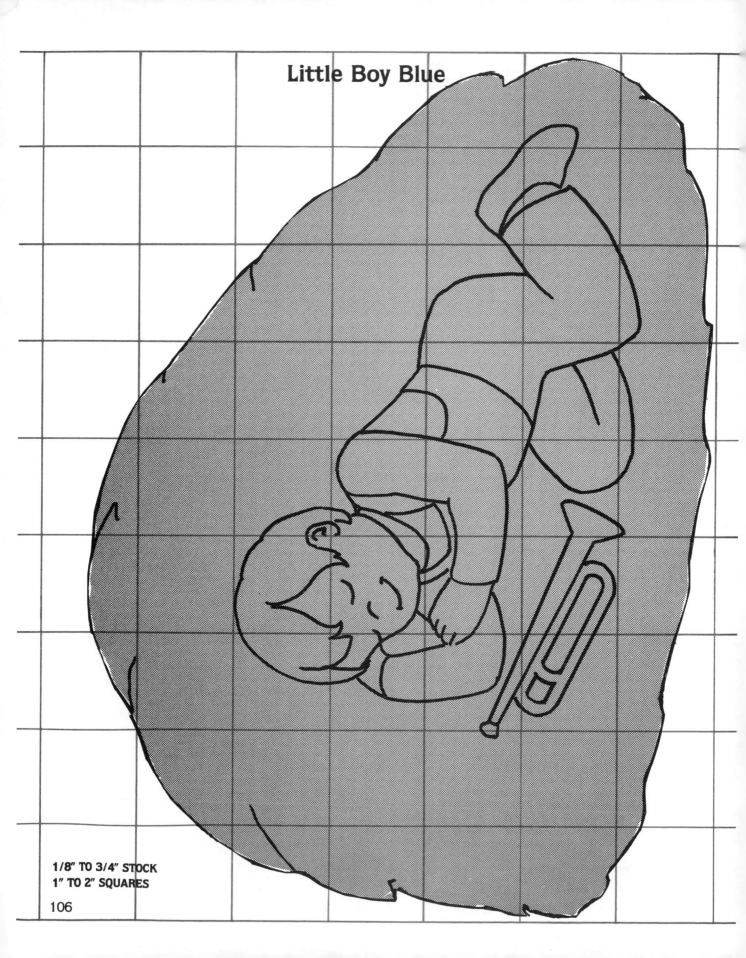

1/8" TO 3/4" STOCK
1" TO 2" SQUARES

106

Jack & Jill

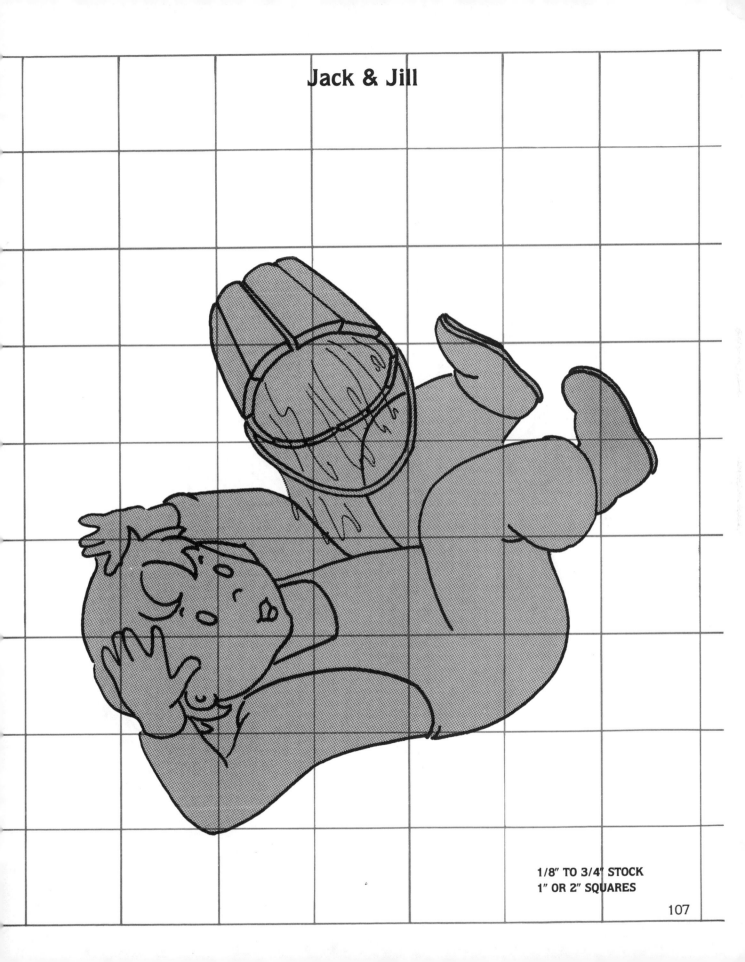

1/8″ TO 3/4″ STOCK
1″ OR 2″ SQUARES

107

1/8" TO 3/4" STOCK
1" TO 2" SQUARES

108

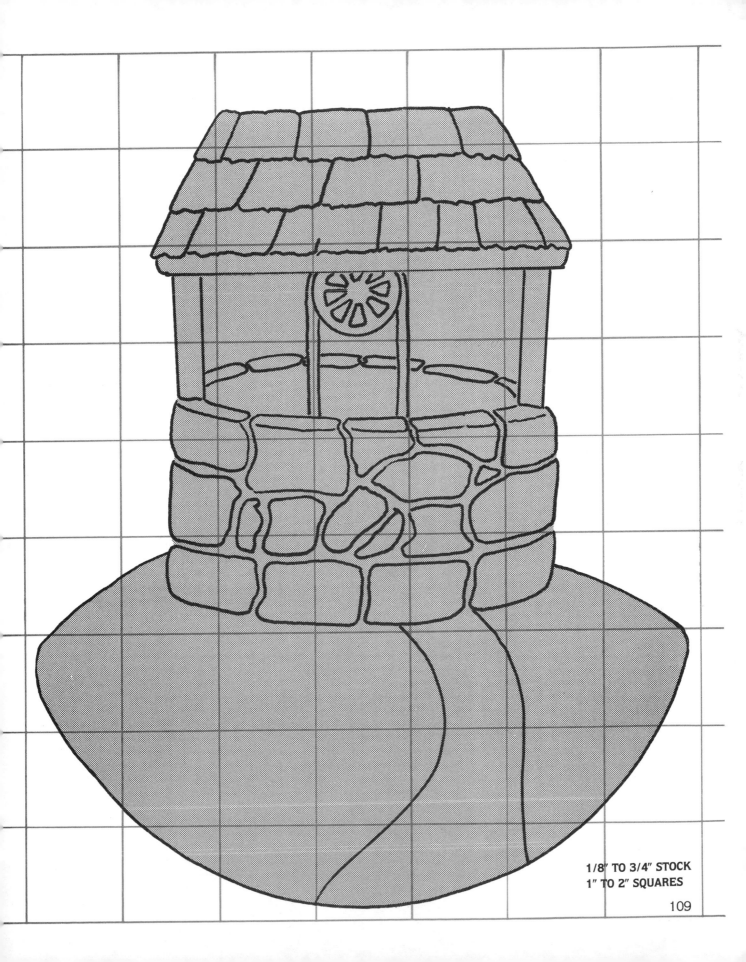

1/8" TO 3/4" STOCK
1" TO 2" SQUARES

109

CHILDREN'S ROOM ACCESSORIES

Teddy Grow Chart

Top a ruled stick with the teddy cut out to create a kiddie grow chart or change teddy shape to a coat rack by drilling holes and inserting dowels or pegs at **X** points.

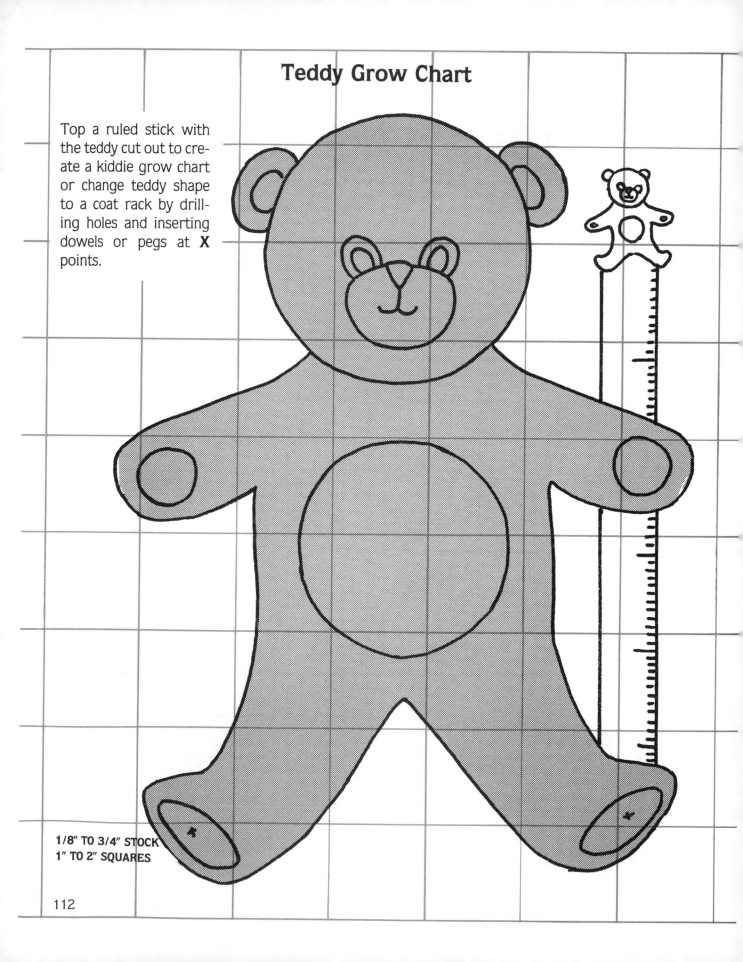

1/8" TO 3/4" STOCK
1" TO 2" SQUARES

ANIMAL CHAIRS

For the two sides, select a design from one of the following pages. Cut the pattern twice out of 3/4" plywood.

Using 3/4" stock cut out back, seat and side supports. Drill 1/8" holes in each support as shown. Attach the seat and back to the side supports using glue and nails or screws. If screws are used, counterbore holes to receive 1-1/4" #8 flathead screws and 3/8" dowel plugs. Mount the two side supports using glue and 1-1/4" #8 roundhead screws.

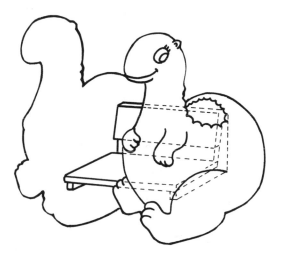

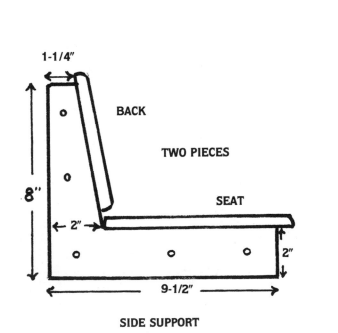

SIDE SUPPORT

BACK

TWO PIECES

SEAT

1-1/4"

8"

2"

9-1/2"

2"

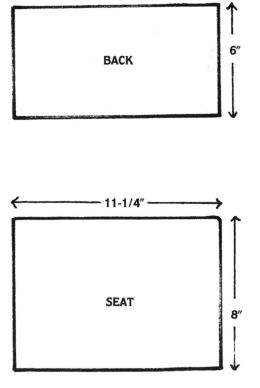

11-1/4"

BACK

6"

11-1/4"

SEAT

8"

Dinosaur Chair

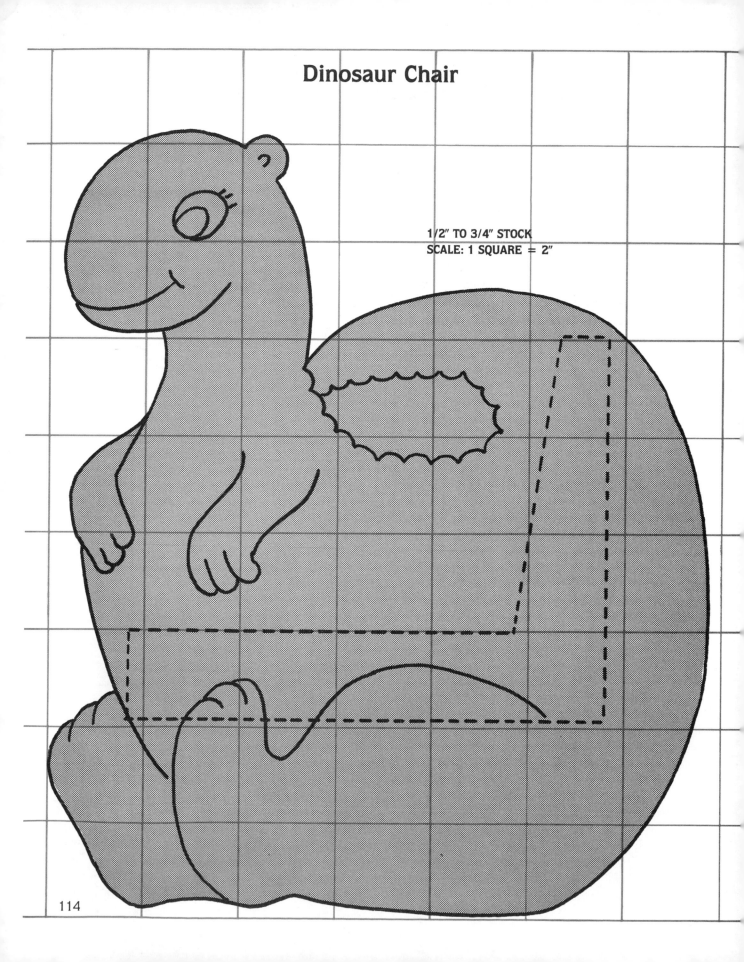

1/2" TO 3/4" STOCK
SCALE: 1 SQUARE = 2"

Sea Lion Chair

1/2" TO 3/4" STOCK
SCALE: 1 SQUARE = 2"

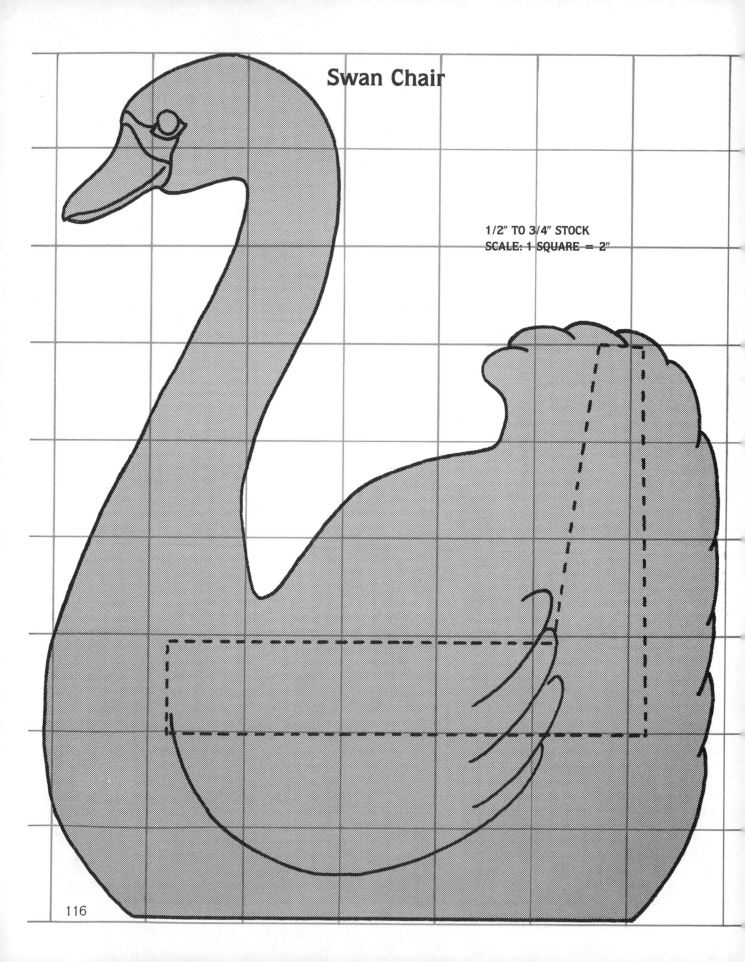

Swan Chair

1/2″ TO 3/4″ STOCK
SCALE: 1 SQUARE = 2″

116

Hippo Chair

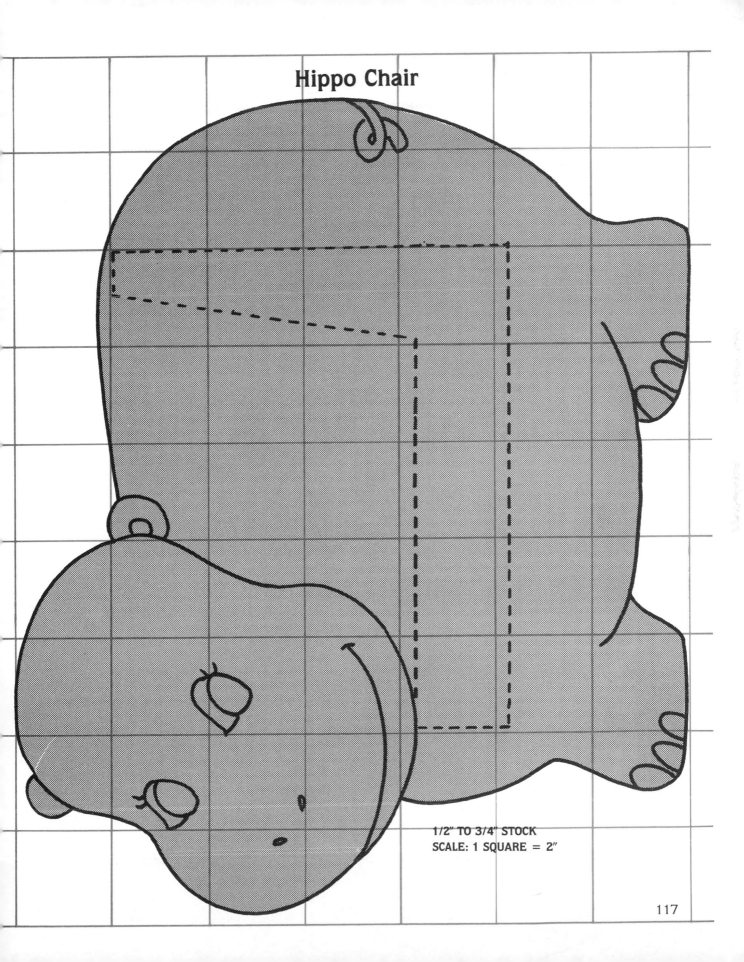

1/2" TO 3/4" STOCK
SCALE: 1 SQUARE = 2"

117

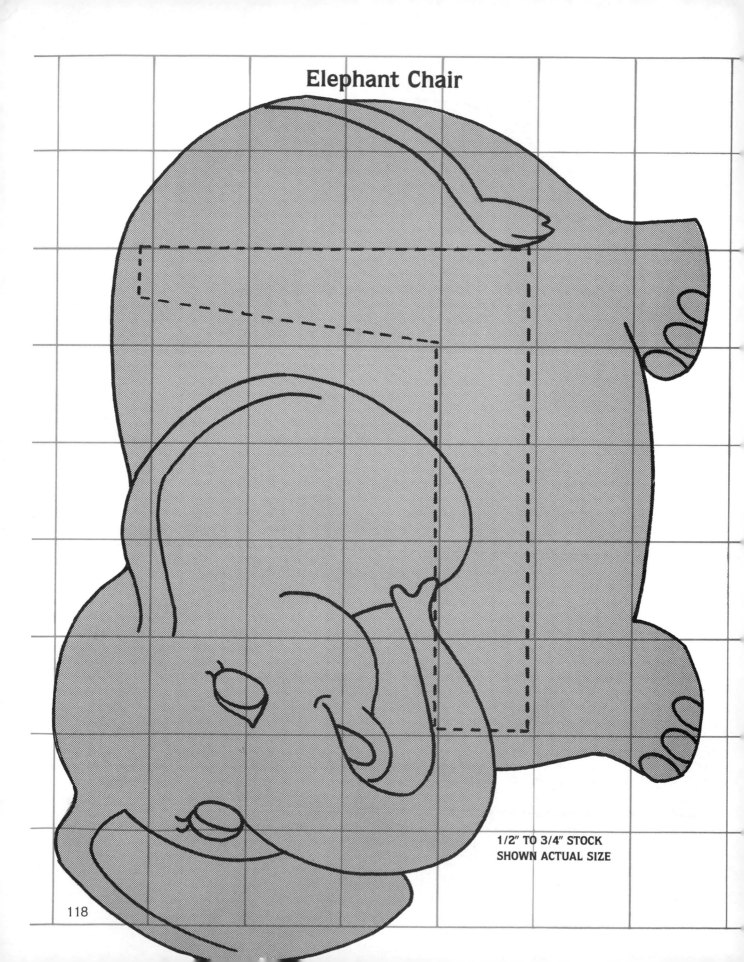

Elephant Chair

1/2" TO 3/4" STOCK
SHOWN ACTUAL SIZE

Dachshund-Scottie Chair

To make a dachshund or scottie chair, use 3/4" stock and let each square of the pattern equal 3". Cut the backrest and round the corners. Cut two outside pieces (with legs), two inside pieces (with head) and four middle pieces.

Fasten the two inside pieces together using glue and four countersunk 1" long #8 flathead screws. Glue the two middle pieces together and repeat for the other two pieces. Glue and nail one set of middle pieces to each side of the inside piece. Fasten the outside piece using glue and four countersunk 1-1/2" #8 flathead screws for each piece. Attach backrest.

Construction Diagram

outside piece
   middle piece
   middle piece
      inside piece
      inside piece
   middle piece
   middle piece
outside piece

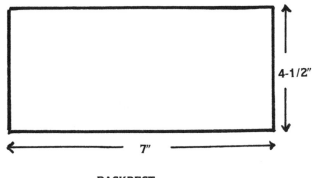

4-1/2"

7"

BACKREST

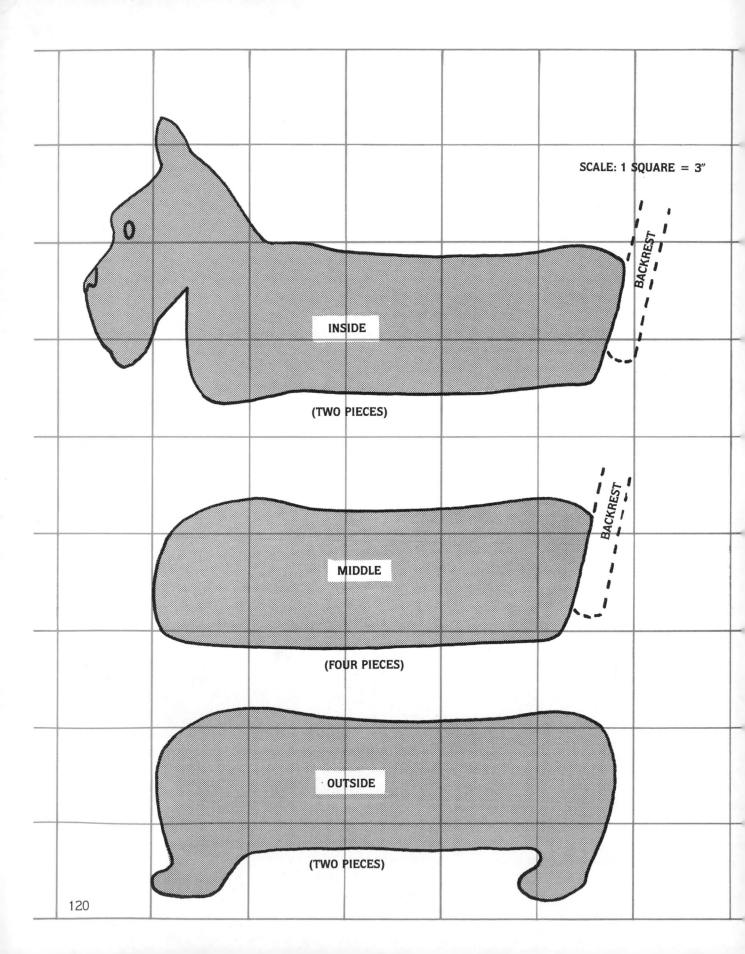

SCALE: 1 SQUARE = 3″

BACKREST

INSIDE

(TWO PIECES)

BACKREST

MIDDLE

(FOUR PIECES)

OUTSIDE

(TWO PIECES)

120

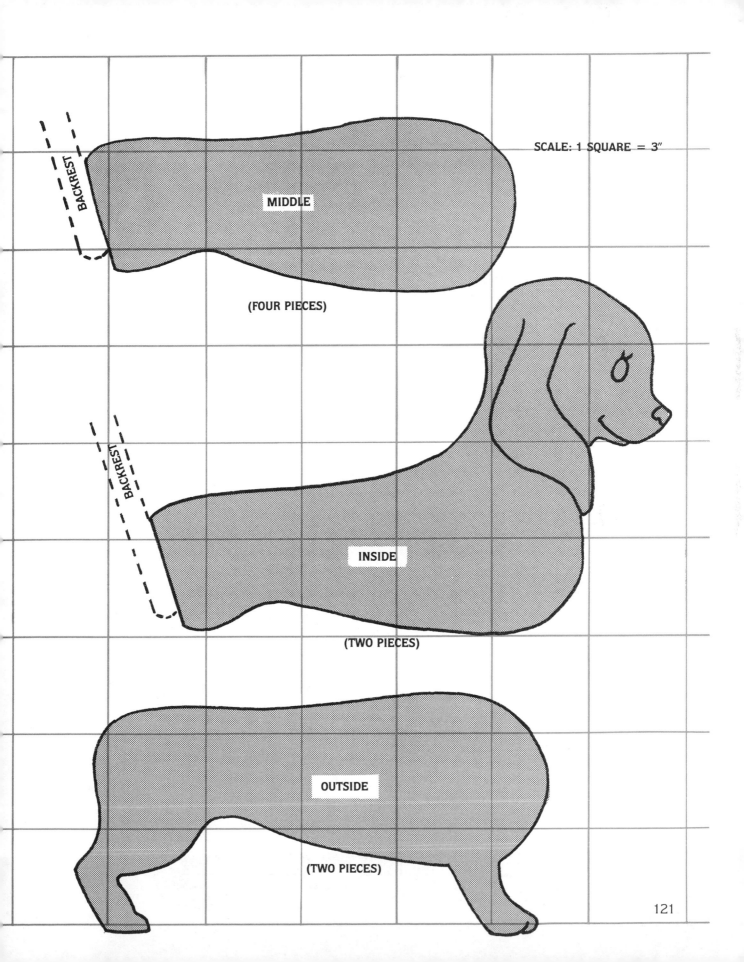

SCALE: 1 SQUARE = 3"

BACKREST

MIDDLE

(FOUR PIECES)

BACKREST

INSIDE

(TWO PIECES)

OUTSIDE

(TWO PIECES)

121

Open Top Cradle

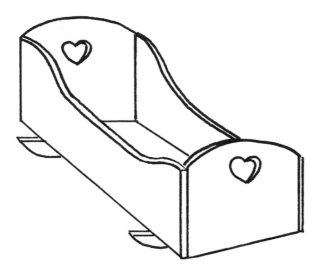

Use 1/4" plywood for bottom and 3/4" stock for all other pieces.

Cut the bottom, sides and end pieces as dimensioned. Using the patterns, cut the two rockers and the heart-shaped holes in the end pieces. Counterbore six holes as shown in each side piece to receive #8 flathead screws. Drill two 1/4" holes 3/4" deep in the bottom edge of each side and the top edge of each rocker. See the figures for the hole locations.

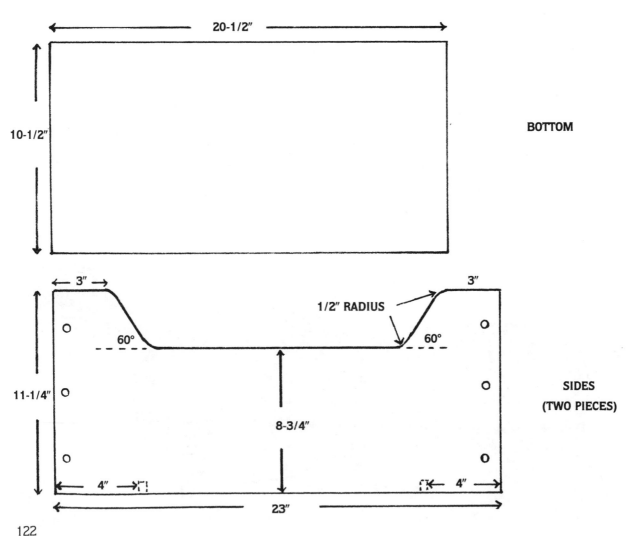

20-1/2"

10-1/2"

BOTTOM

3"

3"

1/2" RADIUS

60°

60°

11-1/4"

8-3/4"

SIDES
(TWO PIECES)

4"

4"

23"

Attach the end pieces to the sides using glue and 1-1/4" #8 flathead screws. Insert 1/4" dowels into the holes in the two rockers, and mate these with the holes in the bottom edge of the two sides. Place the cradle bottom on top of the rockers. Plug the screw holes with 3/8" round-head plugs, glued into place.

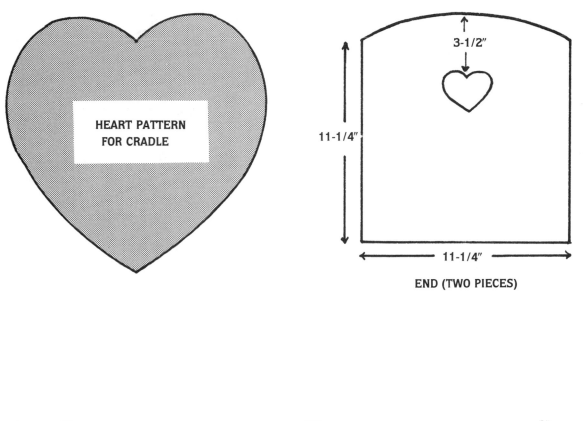

HEART PATTERN FOR CRADLE

END (TWO PIECES)

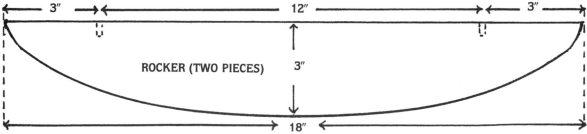

ROCKER (TWO PIECES)

Covered Top Cradle

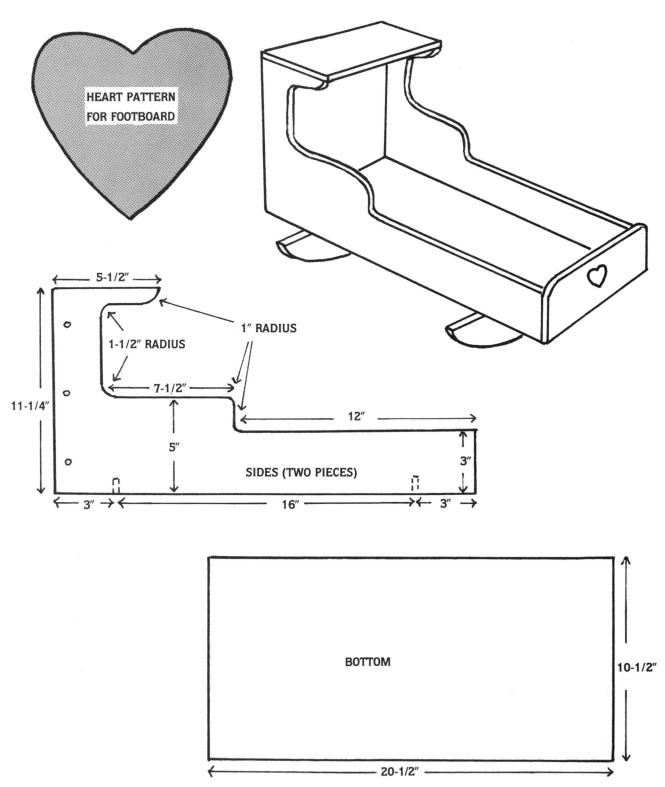

HEART PATTERN FOR FOOTBOARD

5-1/2"

1" RADIUS

1-1/2" RADIUS

7-1/2"

11-1/4"

12"

5"

SIDES (TWO PIECES)

3"

3"

16"

3"

BOTTOM

10-1/2"

20-1/2"

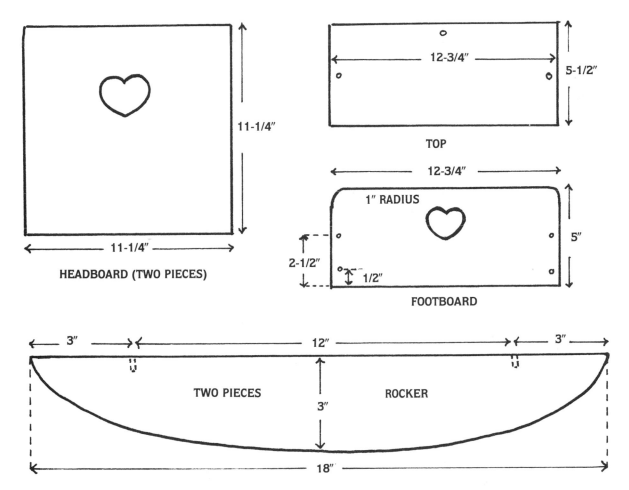

HEADBOARD (TWO PIECES)

11-1/4"

11-1/4"

12-3/4"

5-1/2"

TOP

12-3/4"

1" RADIUS

2-1/2"

1/2"

5"

FOOTBOARD

3"

12"

3"

TWO PIECES

ROCKER

3"

18"

Use 1/4" plywood for the bottom and 3/4" stock for all other pieces. Trace the heart shapes the size shown.

Cut the top, bottom, sides and end pieces as dimensioned. Using the patterns, cut the two rockers and the heart-shaped holes in the end pieces. Counterbore the holes in the top, sides and footboard as shown, to receive #8 flathead screws. Drill two 1/4" holes 3/4" deep in the bottom edge of each side and top edge of each rocker. See the figures for the hole locations.

Attach the end pieces to the sides using glue and 1-1/4" #8 flathead screws. Attach the top to the sides and the headboard. Insert 1/4" dowels into the holes in the two rockers, and mate these with the holes in the bottom edge of the two sides. Place the cradle bottom on top of the rockers. Plug the screw holes with 3/8" round-head plugs, glued into place.

HEART PATTERN
FOR HEADBOARD

Toy Box House

A toy house to keep little treasures, hinged at the top for easy access.

Cut the dormers from 2″ × 4″ stock. Cut all other pieces from 1/2″ plywood. Glue and nail all joints. Sand all pieces carefully and paint in the colors of your choice following the design illustrated. Use H hinges or equivalent plus self-locking lid supports to prevent the lid from accidentally falling.

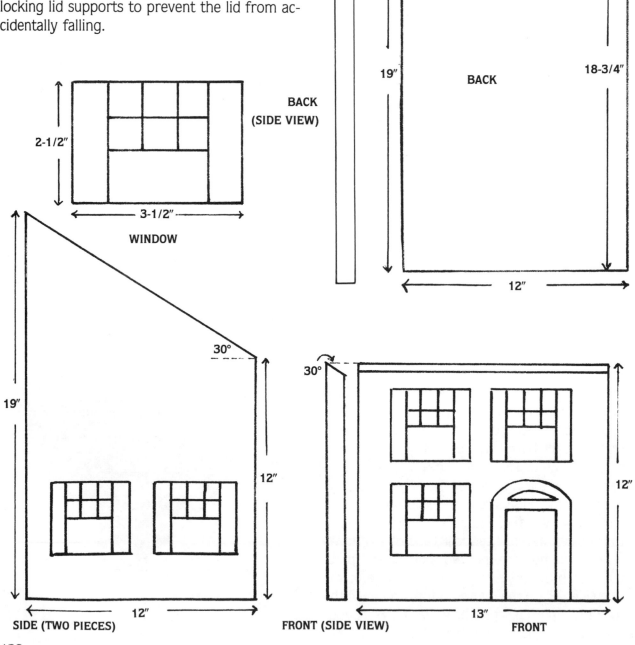

60°

BACK
(SIDE VIEW)

19″

BACK

18-3/4″

12″

2-1/2″

3-1/2″

WINDOW

30°

19″

30°

12″

12″

30°

12″

SIDE (TWO PIECES)

FRONT (SIDE VIEW)

13″

FRONT

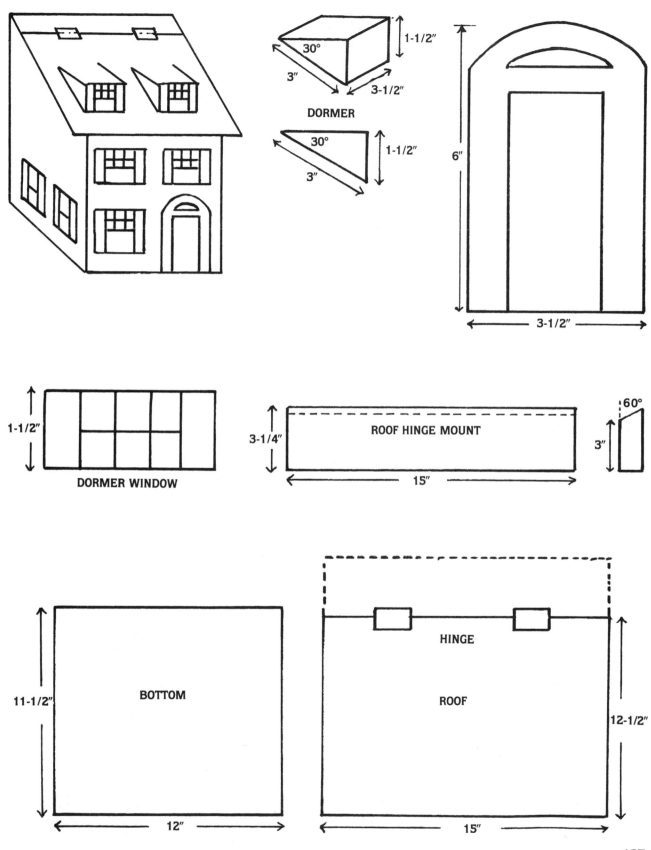

DORMER

DORMER WINDOW

ROOF HINGE MOUNT

BOTTOM

HINGE

ROOF

127

Dual-Style Toy Box

Build your toy box plain or fancy. The plan illustrated can be changed easily to suit either a boy or girl.

Use 3/4" stock. Boards over 11-1/2" wide may be purchased at your lumber yard or created by using dowels and glue. Plywood can also be used.

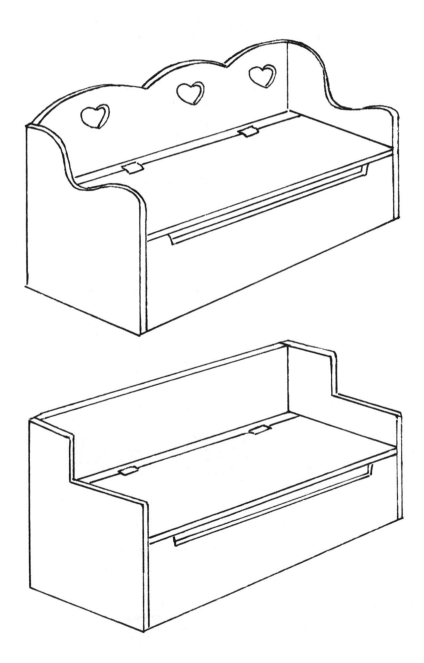

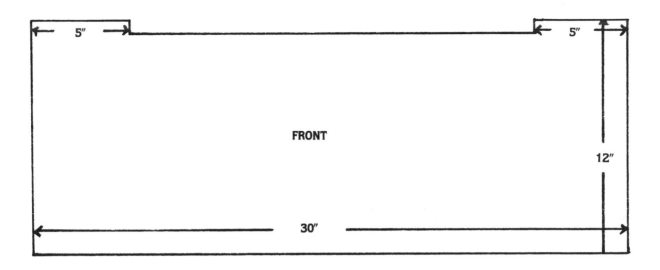

FRONT

5"

5"

12"

30"

CUT ALONG DASHED LINE FOR SQUARE BACK

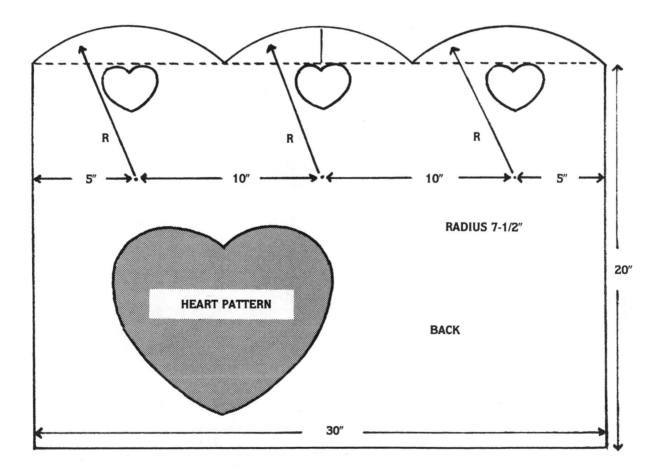

R

R

R

5"

10"

10"

5"

RADIUS 7-1/2"

20"

HEART PATTERN

BACK

30"

129

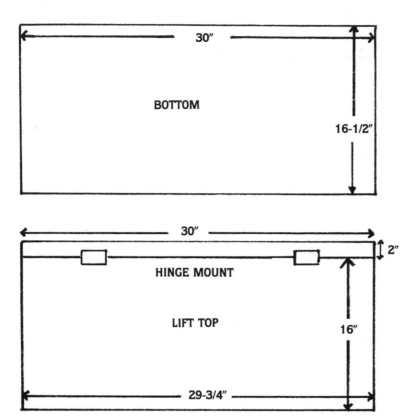

BOTTOM

30″

16-1/2″

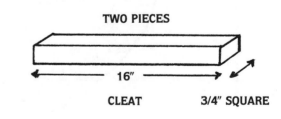

DOWELS

30″

2″

HINGE MOUNT

LIFT TOP

16″

29-3/4″

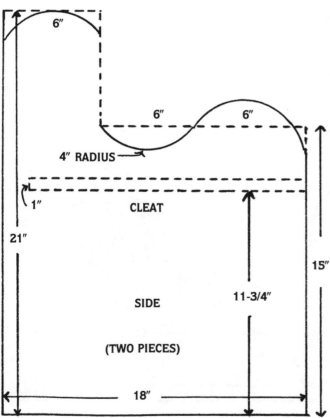

6″

6″   6″

4″ RADIUS

1″

CLEAT

21″

15″

SIDE

11-3/4″

(TWO PIECES)

18″

Cut out all the pieces. When assembling, use glue and nails or glue and 1-1/4″ flathead screws. Countersink screws when installing cleats. Counterbore holes for all other screws and when assembly is complete, fill with dowel plugs. Use H hinges or equivalent plus a self-locking lift top support on each side to prevent it from accidentally falling. The cleats serve to help support the lift top when in the down position.

TWO PIECES

16″

CLEAT   3/4″ SQUARE

Crayon Holder

Cut this little school bus from 2″ × 4″ stock. To hold a box of crayons, drill sixteen 3/8″ holes in the roof of the bus. Trace the bus, and paint as many details as you wish.

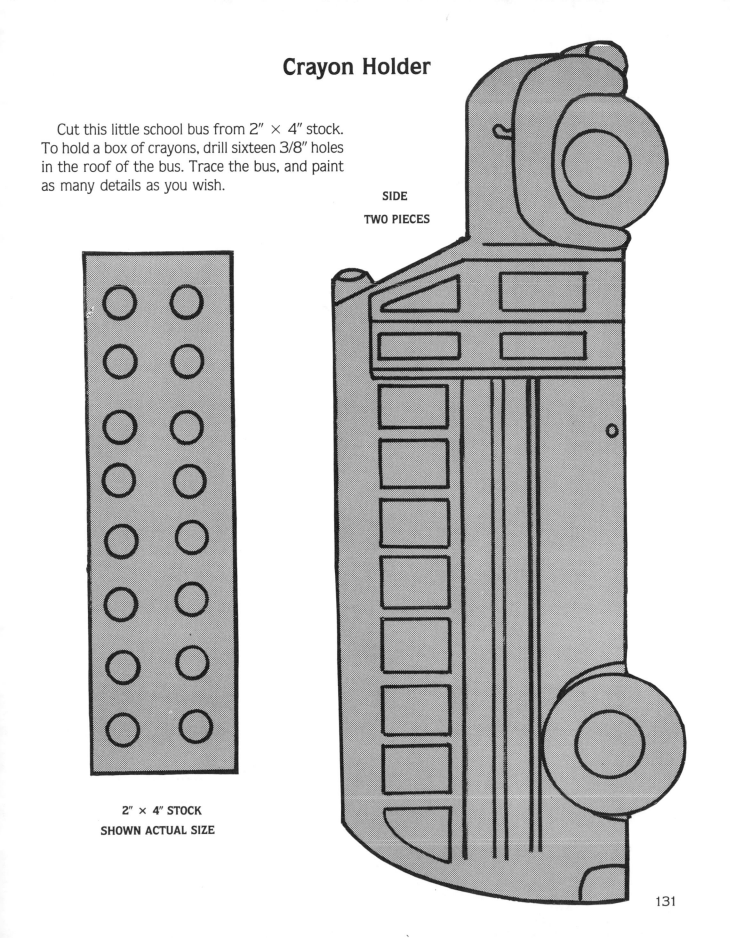

SIDE

TWO PIECES

2″ × 4″ STOCK

SHOWN ACTUAL SIZE

Kiddie Coat Rack

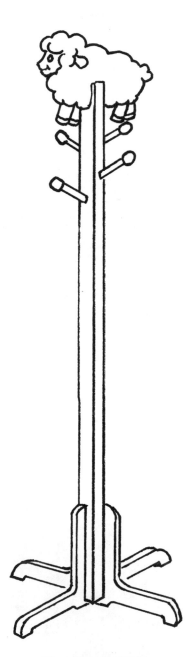

2″ × 2″ × 5′ POST

Select and finish a design from the figures shown throughout the book for the top of the coat rack. The lamb is illustrated on the following page. Cut from 1/4″ plywood.

Use 2″ × 2″ lumber for the post and cut to a length of 5′. Cut a 1/4″ slot in one end of the post. The depth of the cut should be one to two inches. Drill four 3/8″ holes, angled slightly above the horizontal, two to three inches apart as illustrated. One hole should be in each face of the post.

Cut four 5″ lengths from a 3/8″ diameter dowel. Cut four 1″ lengths from a 1″ diameter dowel. Drill a 3/8″ hole approximately 1/2″ deep in one end of each 1″ dowel. Slip a 1″ diameter dowel onto each of the 3/8″ dowels to complete the hangers. Insert hangers in the post and glue.

For the base, cut four pieces of 3/4″ stock or plywood. Drill two 1/8″ holes in each foot piece as shown. Use glue and 2-1/2″ #8 flathead screws to fasten the feet to the post. Attach the decorative design to the post.

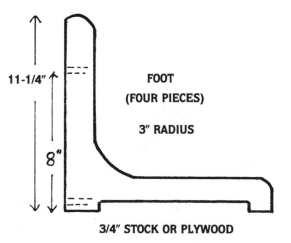

11-1/4″

8″

FOOT

(FOUR PIECES)

3″ RADIUS

3/4″ STOCK OR PLYWOOD

HANGERS
3/8″ DIAMETER DOWELS

SCALE: 1 SQUARE = 2″
1/8″ OR 3/4″ STOCK

KNOBS
1″ DIAMETER DOWELS

5″

(FOUR PIECES)

1″

(FOUR PIECES)

133

Teddy Bear Coat Rack

BASE (END VIEW)

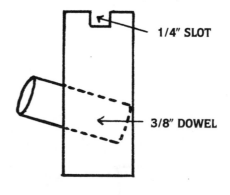

← 1/4" SLOT

← 3/8" DOWEL

Select two teddy bear designs from those illustrated on the followed pages. Cut out of 1/4" plywood and finish to match your decor.

Cut the base piece from 3/4" stock. Cut a 1/4" slot along the top of the base. Drill 3/4" holes as shown, tilted slightly upward. Drill two 1/8" holes through the base, spaced to match the wall studs (usually 16" apart). Use cup washers and ovalhead screws to secure the coat rack to the wall.

Using a 3/8" dia. dowel, cut three pieces 4" long. Insert one dowel piece into each of the three 3/8" holes and glue. Place the bears in the slot on the top of the base piece. Glue if desired.

1/8" TO 3/4" STOCK
1" TO 2" SQUARES

135

1/8" TO 3/4" STOCK
1" TO 2" SQUARES

136

BIRDHOUSES AND WHIRLING BIRDS

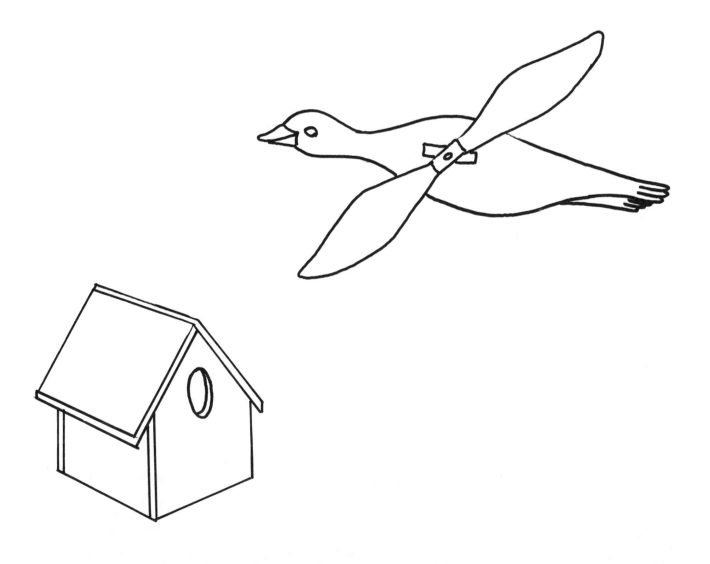

Birdhouses

Included are two easy to make birdhouses that will attract several families of birds. The species which selects your house for a home will depend on the size of the entrance and its height above the floor. Also, it is important for you to mount the birdhouse at the correct height above the ground. The information in the chart below will aid you in making these decisions.

Species	Diameter of Entrance (inches)	Entrance Above Floor (inches)	Height Above Ground (feet)
Bluebird	1 1/2	6	5–10
Chickadees	1 1/8	6–8	6–15
Finch	1 1/2	4–6	5–10
Nuthatch	1 1/4	6–8	5–20
Sparrows (House)	1 1/2	6–8	6–15
Titmouse	1 1/4	6–8	6–15
Woodpecker	2 1/2	10–12	12–20
Wren	1 1/8	2–6	6–10
Barn Swallows	Open		8–12
Robin	Open		6–15
Sparrows (Song)	Open		1–3

Gable Roof Birdhouse

Measurements shown in diagrams below are patterned for 3/4" lumber. If 1/2" thick wood is used, change dimensions to values listed below:

    Front and back are 5 1/2" wide
    Maximum height of sides is 7 1/2"
    Height of left roof is 6"
    Cleats should remain 3/4" square

Drill the entrance hole in the front piece (see table). Secure the front and back to the sides and bottom. Fasten the sides to the bottom. Attach cleats to right and left roof pieces using 1" × #8 screws. Construct roof and set in place.

The cleats are used to position the roof and to serve as a fastener. This is done by drilling a 1/8" hole through the front and back and into the ends of each cleat. Insert a nail in each hole. This also allows for easy removal of the roof for cleaning.

DRILL THREE 1/4" HOLES IN EACH SIDE FOR VENTILATION

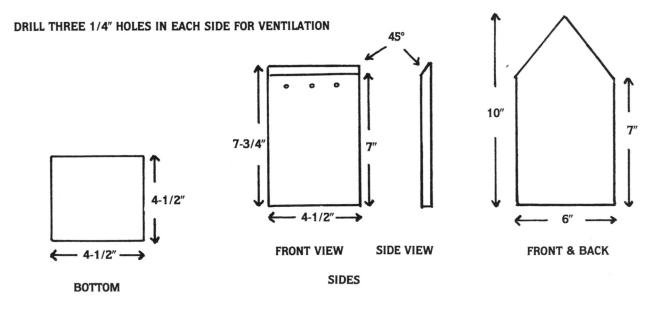

BOTTOM

4-1/2"
4-1/2"

7-3/4"
4-1/2"
7"
45°
FRONT VIEW   SIDE VIEW

SIDES

TWO PIECES

10"
7"
6"
FRONT & BACK

TWO PIECES

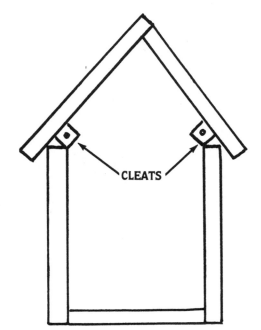

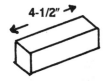

3/4″ SQUARE

CLEAT

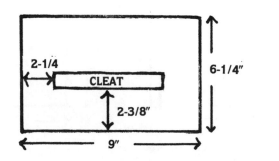

LEFT ROOF TOP

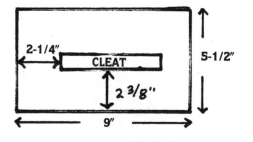

RIGHT ROOF TOP

140

Slant Roof Birdhouse

NOTE: Diagram measurements below are dimensioned for 3/4" thick lumber. If 1/2" thick wood is used, change the dimensions to the values listed below:

Front is 5 1/2" wide

Reduce 7 7/16" dimension of roof to 7 1/4"

Increase height of front from 10" to 10 1/8"

Drill the entrance hole in the front piece. (See Table) Attach the cleats to the roof as shown, using two 1-1/4" × No. 8 screws. Fasten the sides to the bottom. Secure the front to the sides and bottom.

Attach the back to the sides and bottom using 1-1/4" × #8 flathead screws. Use two or three screws for each side and two for the bottom. These should be countersunk. Mount roof by forcing it to be flush with the back. Drill two 1/8" holes through each side and the cleats. Insert a nail through each hole. This serves as the fastener and also allows easy removal for cleaning.

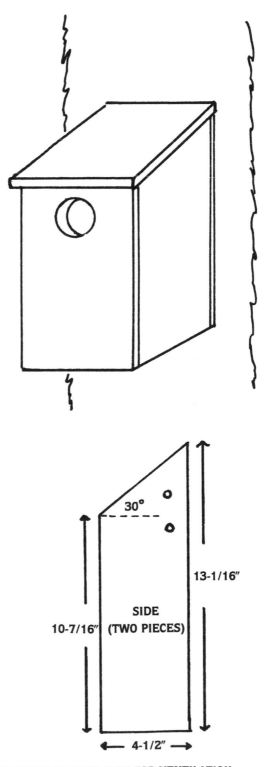

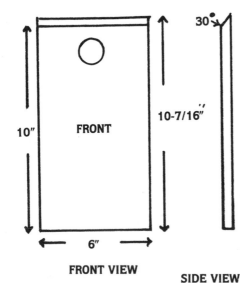

FRONT VIEW   SIDE VIEW

DRILL TWO 1/4" HOLES IN EACH SIDE FOR VENTILATION.

141

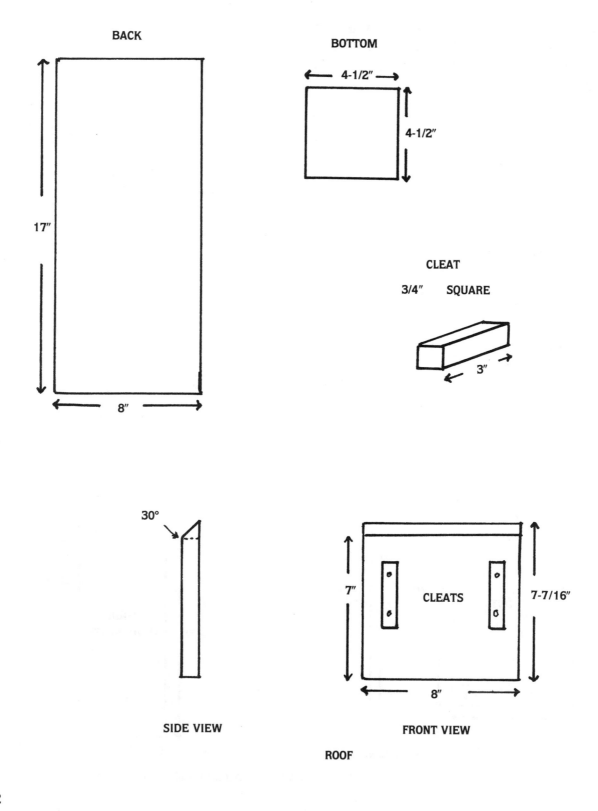

BACK

BOTTOM

4-1/2"

4-1/2"

17"

8"

CLEAT

3/4"   SQUARE

3"

30°

CLEATS

7"

7-7/16"

8"

SIDE VIEW

FRONT VIEW

ROOF

142

Whirling Birds

The whirling birds or *whirligigs* are constructed in three parts: the body, the wing and the wing support. Patterns for both large and small species are included. Those for the large species must be enlarged (directions are on page 10) while the smaller ones can be traced as shown. The wing supports can be made as illustrated on the following pages, or they can be made of dowels. Should you prefer to use dowels, follow the instructions below.

Cut a dowel long enough to extend through the body of the bird and to serve as a spacer on each side of the body (4-3/4" for large birds and 1-1/2" for the small birds). Drill a hole through the body which has the same diameter as the dowel. The position of the hole should be at the approximate center of gravity. This point is found by balancing the body on your finger or on the edge of a board and then measuring at this point about halfway from the bottom to the top of the bird.

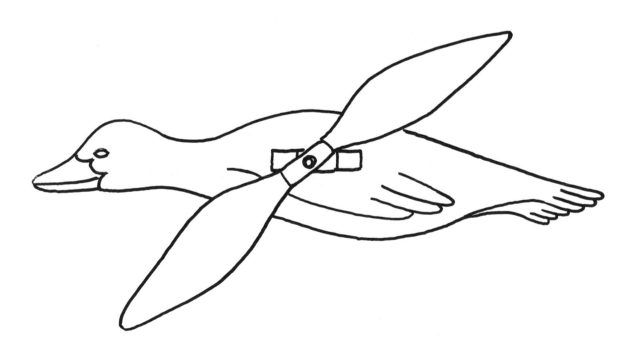

The Large Whirling Bird

Cut the body piece, two wing pieces, two wing base pieces and two wing support pieces. Select desired body from illustrations beginning on page 147. Use 3/4" lumber for all the pieces except the wings. For these use 3/16" or 1/4" plywood.

Find the center of the wing base piece and drill a 5/16" hole. If you choose to use a metal sleeve, enlarge the hole to equal the outside diameter of the sleeve. Draw a diagonal on each end of the wing base pieces and cut a 3/4" deep slot.

WING BASE (TWO PIECES)

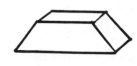

WING SUPPORT (TWO PIECES)

WING (FOUR PIECES)

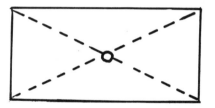

WING BASE PIECE WITH HOLE

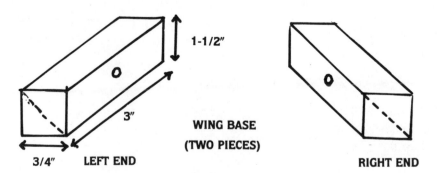

1-1/2"

3"

3/4"   **LEFT END**

WING BASE (TWO PIECES)

RIGHT END

Holding Fixture

To hold the base pieces in the proper position when sawing (with a radial or table saw), first cut a holding fixture similar to the one pictured. Cut the holes in the holding fixture the same size as the slotted ends of the wing base pieces. Insert the wing base piece into the right hole and cut the slot. Turn the base over and insert it in the same hole and cut the slot. Repeat for the second wing base piece using the left hole. The width of the slots in the ends should be slightly less than the thickness of your sanded 1/4" thick plywood wings. Use moisture-resistant glue and a 1/2" finishing nail to fasten the wings to the base.

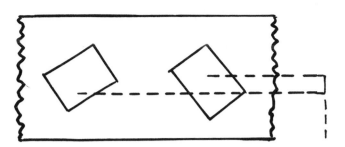

SLOTS FOR WING BASE PIECES.

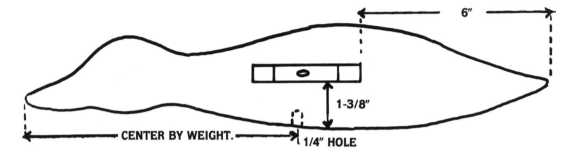

6"

1-3/8"

CENTER BY WEIGHT. — 1/4" HOLE

Wing Support

Drill a 3/16" pilot hole in each wing support piece about 1" deep. Fasten the support to the body, using glue and nails. Drill a 1/4" hole 1" deep in the underside of the bird for the pivot rod. Use a 1/4" lag screw to fasten the wing to the support. Use a washer on each side of the wing base. Mount the second wing so it is the mirrow image of the first one. This ensures that the two wings will turn in opposite directions.

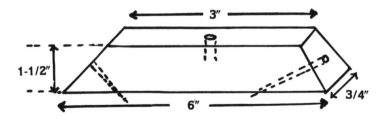

3"

1-1/2"

6"

3/4"

USE 1/4" FINISHING NAIL.

WING SUPPORT

145

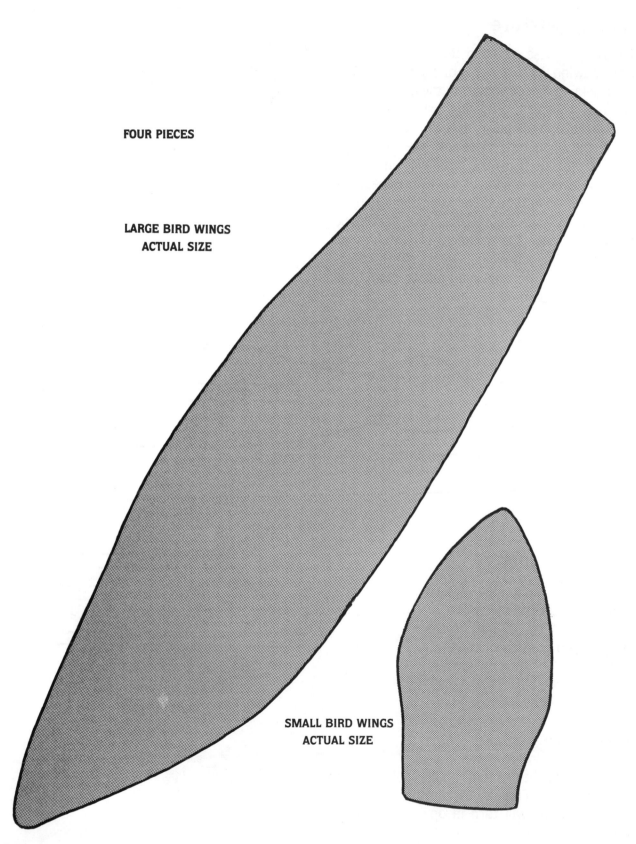

FOUR PIECES

LARGE BIRD WINGS
ACTUAL SIZE

SMALL BIRD WINGS
ACTUAL SIZE

The Small Whirling Birds

Cut the body piece, two wing pieces, two wing base pieces, and two 1" diameter dowels 1/4" long for spacers. Select the desired bird body style from the following pages. Find the center of the wing base piece and drill a 3/16" hole. Use 3/4" lumber for the body and wing base pieces, and 1/4" outside plywood for the wings.

Cut two spacer pieces from a 1" diameter dowel long enough to insure the wings will not strike the body when they are rotating (1/4" to 1/2" should do). Drill a hole through each dowel piece using a drill bit larger than the screw you plan to use to fasten the wings to the body. Draw a diagonal line on each end of the wing base pieces and cut a 3/8" deep slot.

To hold the base pieces in the proper position when sawing (using a radial or table saw), first cut a holding fixture similar to the one pictured. Cut the holes in the holding fixture the same size as the slotted ends of the wing base pieces. Insert the wing base piece into the right hole and cut the slot. Turn the base over and insert it in the same hole and cut the slot. Repeat for the second wing base piece using the left hole. The width of the slots in the ends should be slightly less than the thickness of your sanded 1/4" thick plywood wings. Use moisture-resistant glue and a 1/2" finishing nail to fasten the wings to the base.

SLOTS FOR WING BASES

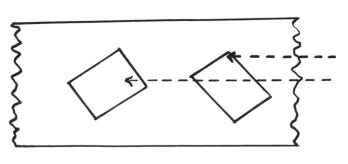

HOLDING FIXTURE

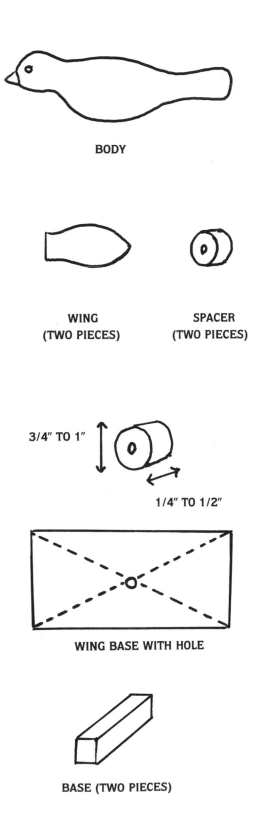

BODY

**WING
(TWO PIECES)**

**SPACER
(TWO PIECES)**

3/4" TO 1"

1/4" TO 1/2"

WING BASE WITH HOLE

BASE (TWO PIECES)

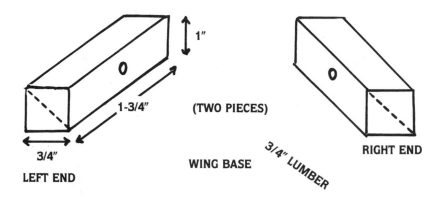

1"

1-3/4"

3/4"

(TWO PIECES)

WING BASE

3/4" LUMBER

RIGHT END

LEFT END

Find the center of the small bird of your choice by balancing the body cut-out shape on your finger. Drill a 1/4" hole on the underside of the body, 1" deep, for the pivot rod. Drill a 1/8" pilot hole on each side of the body, 1" from the top of the bird's body, at the balanced center, as shown.

Mount the wing to the body using a 1-1/4" #8 screw on each side. Place a washer on either side of the wing. To ensure the wings will turn in opposite directions, mount the second wing so it is the mirror image of the first.

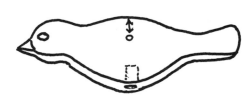

PILOT HOLE

BALANCE
CENTER

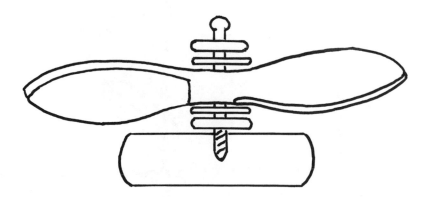

ROUND-HEAD SCREW

SPACER

WASHER

WING

WASHER

SPACER

BODY

Stork

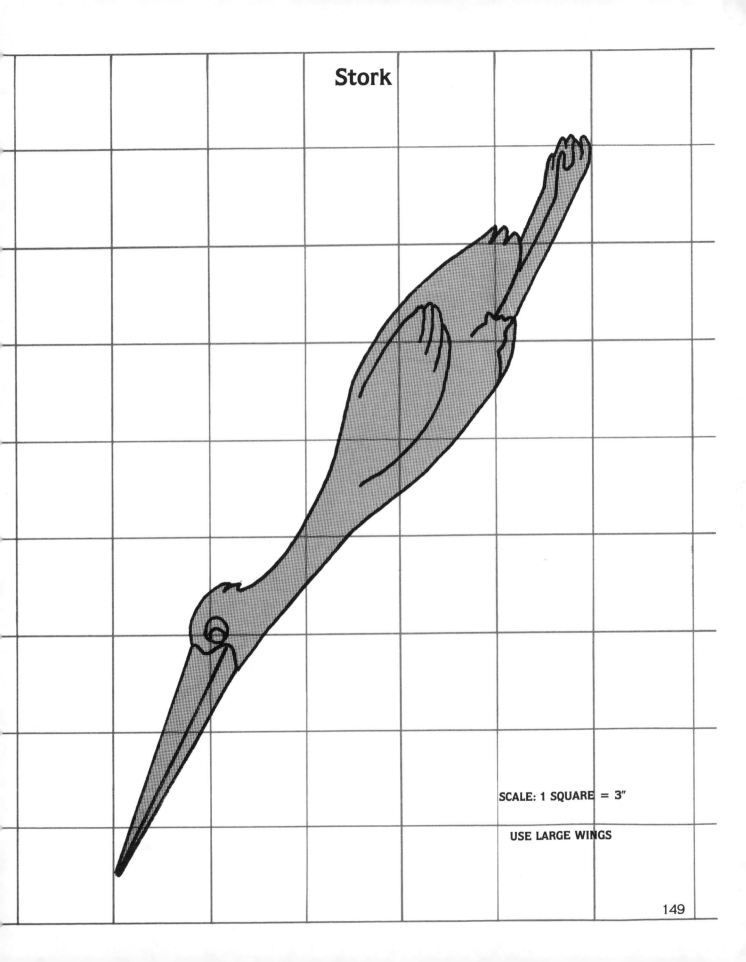

SCALE: 1 SQUARE = 3″

USE LARGE WINGS

149

Roadrunner

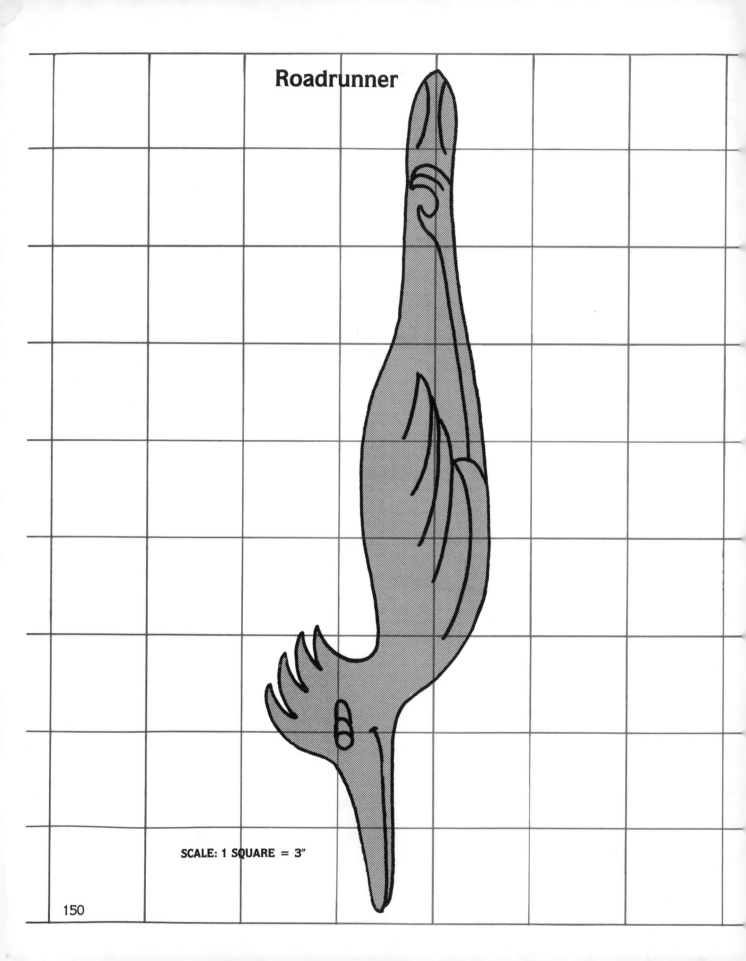

SCALE: 1 SQUARE = 3"

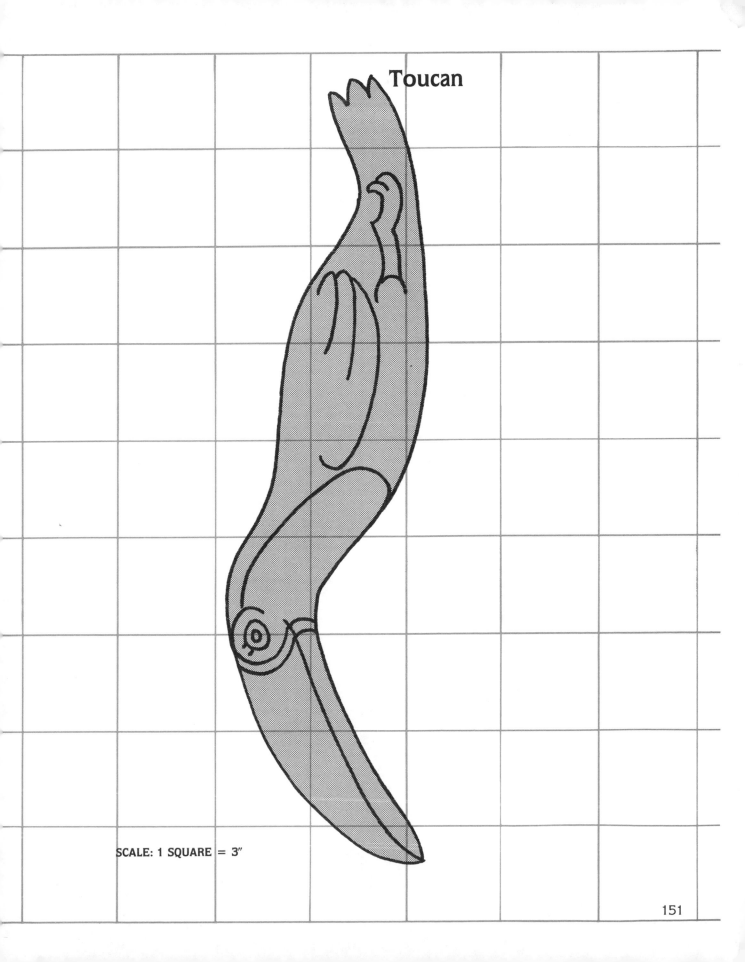

Toucan

SCALE: 1 SQUARE = 3″

Goose

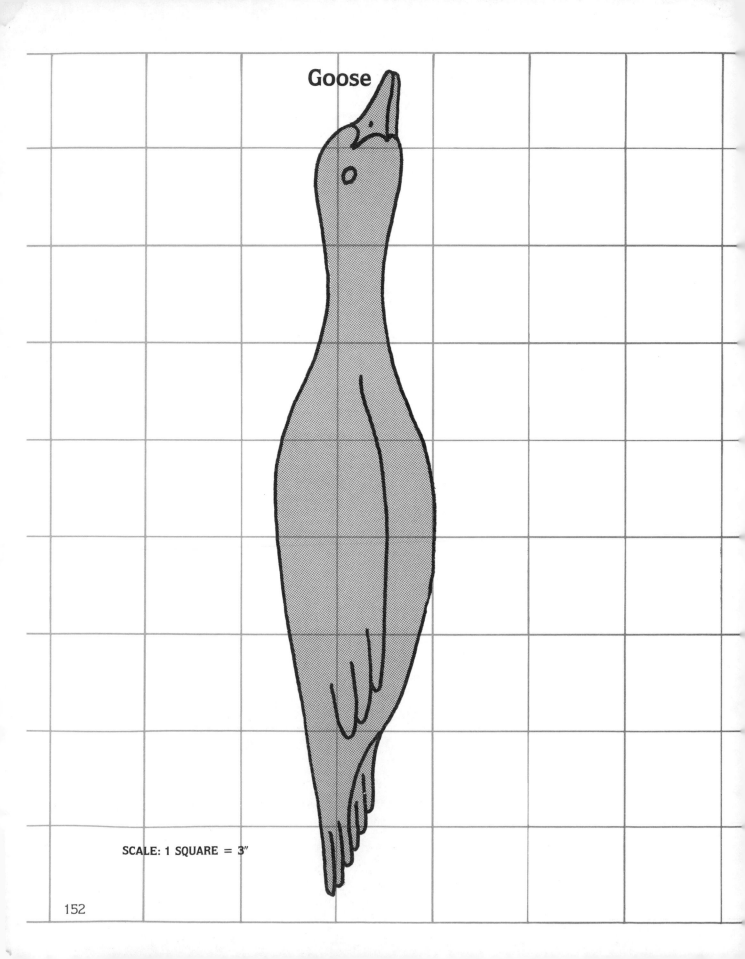

SCALE: 1 SQUARE = 3″

Pelican

SCALE: 1 SQUARE = 3″

Sparrow

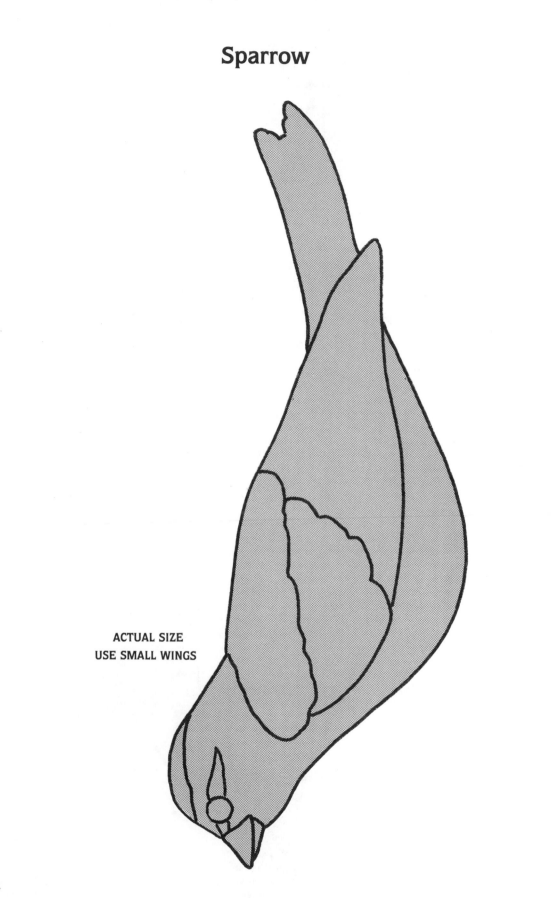

**ACTUAL SIZE
USE SMALL WINGS**

Robin

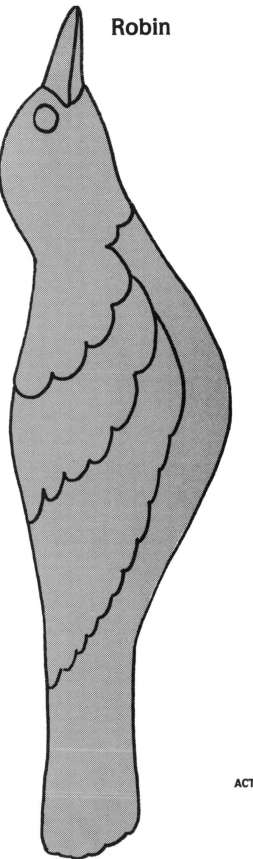

ACTUAL SIZE

155

Macaw

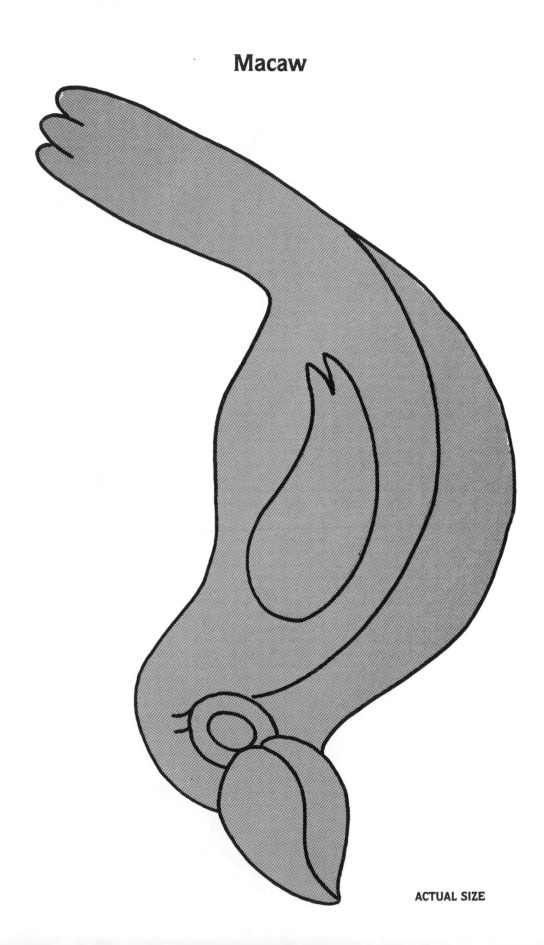

ACTUAL SIZE

Owl

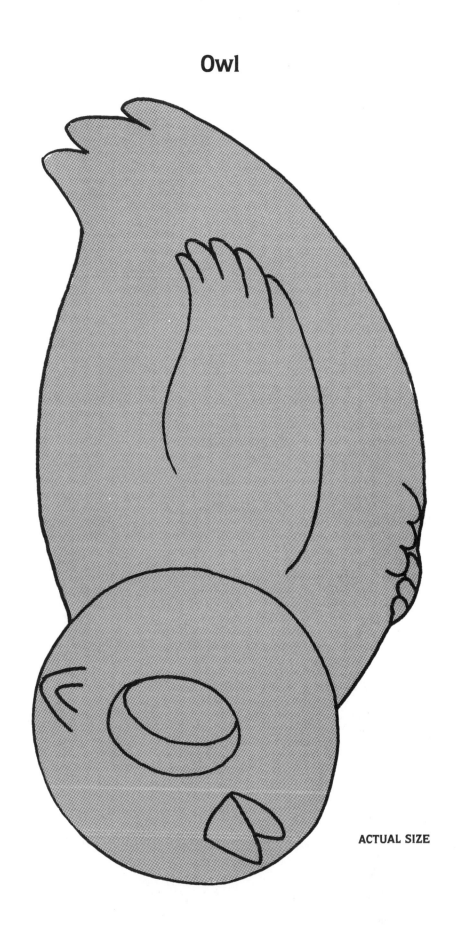

ACTUAL SIZE

Kingfisher

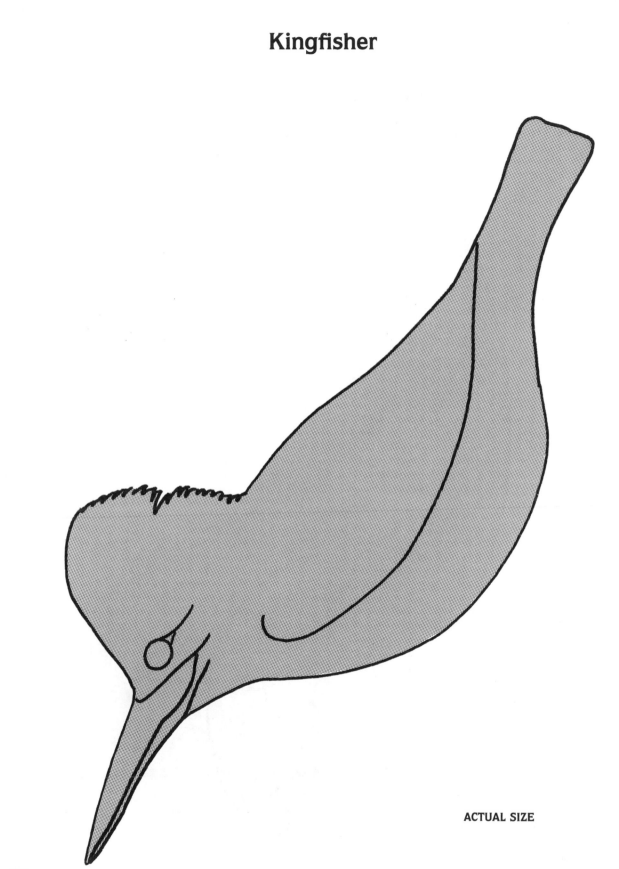

ACTUAL SIZE

INDEX